LOVE
AT
WORK

LOVE
AT
WORK

Margaret Kent
and Robert Feinschreiber

WARNER BOOKS

A Warner Communications Company

Copyright © 1988 Margaret Kent & Robert Feinschreiber

Warner Books, Inc., 666 Fifth Avenue, New York, NY 10103
A Warner Communications Company

Book Design by Nick Mazzella

Printed in the United States of America

First printing: Septermber 1988

10 9 8 7 6 5 4 3 2 1

Library of Congress Cataloging-in-Publication Data

Kent, Margaret, 1942–
  Love at work / Margaret Kent & Robert Feinschreiber.
     p.   cm.

  1. Mate selection—United States.   2. Dating (Social customs)
3. Employment of men—United States.   4. Love.   I. Feinschreiber,
Robert.   II. Title.
HQ801.K48   1988
646.7′7—dc19   88-14902
   ISBN 0-446-51469-1   CIP

To our parents,
Hilda and Jack Bradfield
Maxine and Selven Feinschreiber

Acknowledgments

This book owes its existence, in large part, to the many readers of *How to Marry the Man of Your Choice* who so persistently wrote to us to say how busy they were at work, to tell us how little time they had to socialize, and to ask our help in finding love at work.

We received a great deal of assistance and encouragement from our colleagues at Warner Books, and are especially grateful to our original editor, Bob Miller, and our subsequent editor, Nansey Neiman.

Our agent, Sandra Choron, and her associate, Trish Todd, have also been very helpful in making this book a reality.

Three people helped us put this book together, though at times it must have seemed to them like an internship in the deciphering of hieroglyphics. We take this opportunity to show our gratitude to Alan Layng, Doreen Perry, and Alvaro Zayas.

A number of people furnished us with their thoughts and comments concerning *Love at Work.* We thank them all, especially Lari Levey, Kathryn Feinschreiber, Sharon Clifford, Steven Feinschreiber, and most especially Selven Feinschreiber, for their useful suggestions.

Contents

Preface

When I first went to work after high school, I didn't have the opportunity to analyze jobs in terms of their husband-hunting potential. I needed a job quickly as dozens of relatives were descending upon us after Castro took over Cuba. I went to work for the telephone company as a long-distance operator. There were more than a thousand operators, all of whom were women.

With odds like these, anything is an improvement. After college I became a high school teacher, but male faculty and staff were few. Then I became more conscious of what it takes to meet and marry, and I began teaching adult education in the evenings. I met my first husband when he was a student in my Spanish class. He was an attorney and a physician, and was looking to expand his skills and horizons.

Later, after my first husband died, I went to law school and became an attorney. It was through these activities that I met Bob Feinschreiber, who is now my husband. He is both an attorney and a CPA, and we used business gatherings to develop our personal relationship.

Thus, learning to select a job and learning to use my job as a source of dates and mates was a gradual process.

You can benefit from my experiences as well as my academic research, and use your job more effectively to meet the man of your choice.

—Margaret Kent

My earliest jobs brought me in contact with few, if any, women. I delivered flowers when I was a high school freshman, but it seemed like everyone was sending condolences. Then I became a research assistant in civil engineering at New York University, where none of my co-workers was female.

Years later, when I reentered the business world after teaching accounting at Yale and law at Wayne State, the situation was disheartening. I wanted a woman who was a colleague, not a woman who was willing to settle for a subservient position. Neither Chrysler nor Seagrams, my first two corporate employers, would hire women in managerial or professional capacities, and the CPA firm for which I went to work was no better.

I would not have fulfilled my personal goals if Margaret Kent hadn't taken the initiative and met me.

—Robert Feinschreiber

We work together and play together. Our relationship grew because we share both personal goals and professional interests. We practice law together, make love together, travel together, and grow together. Now we have written a book together so that you can share some of our happiness.

—Margaret Kent
—Robert Feinschreiber

LOVE
AT
WORK

Introduction

An increasing number of women are finding love at work because they're too busy to find love anywhere else and because they recognize the many advantages to meeting men on their jobs or through their jobs. This trend is continuing and strengthening, but has only recently begun to attract the attention of scholars, professionals, and the media.

During the past few years, we've been traveling extensively in response to the great interest in *How to Marry the Man of Your Choice*. We've been speaking with women everywhere who want marriage, but don't want to put their careers on hold while they look for mates.

You can have both a husband and a career, and these two goals can reinforce each other if you find love at work. You can have it all—love and money, happiness and success, the bedroom and the boardroom. You just want to know how. It is for you that the book is written.

Motherly advice often fails to meet the needs of the present generation of single women. Society has changed so greatly that advice which was once so useful is now useless or worse. Women need new skills, new attitudes, and new answers if they're looking to marry for life. We hope that *Love at Work* will help you reach this goal.

ISSUES AND OPPORTUNITIES

More women are working—and in higher positions—than ever before. They have contact with men that was inconceivable just a few generations ago, yet closer contact doesn't necessarily bring about better relationships.

Early career women emphasized their jobs to the exclusion of other goals. They made it clear that they were working to build their careers, not to look for husbands, so they avoided marriage and other entangling relationships. They struggled so hard to establish their own credentials and respect that they wouldn't take any chances "fooling around" at work.

Battle of the Sexes

During the long fight for women's rights, a number of women have come to view *all* men as the enemy. Women who hold this point of view object to love at work and to dating and marriage in general because they view these relationships as fraternizing with the enemy. And if you're looking for love at work, they accuse you of being a traitor to their cause. They're too strident for their own good, and most important, they're too strident for yours.

By now, the battle of the sexes should have ended. Everyone should have declared victory and gone off into the sunset, each of you with the person of your choice. But the battle of the sexes didn't end; it merely moved inside to the corporate offices. In fact, the rapid (or slow, depending upon your point of view) movement of women into the corporate hierarchy has merely changed the balance of power.

You're harmed by the battle of the sexes because the cross fire of that battle can reduce your chances for happiness. Many people, both men and women, have decided to stop fighting and seek a private peace with a member of the opposite sex. This is the strategy you should be following if you're seeking love at work.

Career opportunities are there. Grab them. Men also are there. Grab them too. As far as the battle of the sexes is concerned, it's time to make love, not war.

Fighting the Sexual Stereotypes

If you're serious about finding love at work, you've got to recognize the stereotypes created by the hate-mongers of each sex. Then you can move beyond the stereotypes and discover people as they really are.

Women who hate men claim that men make passes at them solely to demean them or keep them in their places as objects of carnal desire. In reality, men often make passes at their female colleagues because they haven't yet learned how to approach women whom they'll be seeing on a recurring basis. Men who hate women claim female executives use relationships and sex to get ahead. In reality, these women are often workaholics who have put relationships and sex on the back burner.

Some men still assume that a woman won't work if she marries or that she'll have children, then quit. Some women still feel that they have to work twice as hard and avoid relationships with men to prove that love and marriage aren't overwhelming their career goals. One stereotype begets the other, and both are equally erroneous.

Corporate Sexism

Many companies are segregated—not by race, but by sex. Often you can't even see the segregation unless you look closely, but sexual segregation pervades companies with strong anti-love attitudes. Look at the peer groups as well as the formal structure. The company that began with an old-boy network now has an old-girl network too. Such a company had male sexists who hate women, and still does, but now it also has female sexists who hate men.

Male sexism has received considerable attention in recent years. Its harm to corporate productivity and the image of corporate fairness has long been documented. Another form of sexism that is equally harmful, but largely ignored by the media, is female sexism.

If you're serious about finding love at work, look for a company that opposes all forms of sexism—male sexism and female sexism alike. Look for telltale signs of sexual segregation. At a minimum, visit the employee cafeteria and see if everyone is having lunch with someone of the same gender. Find out whether the female executives have normal relationships with men, including dating, sex, and marriage. Also find out about the relationships that male executives have with women, and whether their wives have careers of their own.

Lace Curtain

Some women in power have anti-male attitudes. As they move up in the corporate hierarchy, they show their disdain for men and their contempt for women who like men. They spurn concepts that favor relationships between men and women, and even oppose cooperation or collaboration across the gender boundary. They create a lace curtain that screens out men and excludes women like you who are favorably inclined toward men. If you're looking for love at work, avoid companies where you find this lace curtain.

The lace curtain is especially easy to find in certain women's magazines and in some of the very large elitist newspapers. Their articles on relationships have a common theme—"blame the man." But you should be smart enough to know that there are men who love too much, and women who can't love.

The Corporate Chaperone

Businesses that make rules against love at work create an environment that favors those who find these rules easy to obey. These companies act as if they're seeking the corporate eunuch, someone who eschews all thoughts of love and sex, at least during work hours. They prefer to hire the ultra-celibate rather than face the consequences of human attraction. Their rules give an edge to women who hate men and men who hate women since they're not looking to date people of the opposite sex at work. The rest of us are supposed to ignore our sex drives, our impetus to procreate, and our potential feelings of love we are looking to give someone.

Businesses with anti-dating rules are creating an environment in which normal people cannot be hardworking if they're single. If they devote large segments of time to their job, but are prohibited from finding love at work, they don't have time to socialize outside of work, so they can't find someone to love. Normal single people eventually find this situation intolerable and will move elsewhere. The company will lose many of its most energetic workers.

Let your company know that if it wants normal women and normal men, it must give them a chance to act normal.

JOB HUNTING AND HUSBAND HUNTING

Most guides to dating and husband-hunting focus on food, fashion, and sex, assuming the woman has endless free time to pursue her future mate. This book realizes that she is building a career, and that marriage is only one of her priorities.

Most guides to career selection and job hunting focus on money and power and emphasize factors such as compensation and career advancement. They overlook the importance of interpersonal relationships in general, and husband-hunting in particular, in career development and job selection.

If you're just finishing school and entering the workforce, this book can help you choose your career wisely. If you're already working, the book can help you choose the right job. In either case, *Love at Work* will show you how to use your job wisely.

If you're helping other people move forward in their careers, you can use this material to aid them in evaluating the social aspects of a particular career or job opportunity.

This book is written primarily for women, but much of the advice is equally useful for men. Finding love at work is a terrific opportunity for men, as it is for women, but it requires planning and perseverance, as well as a positive attitude on your part.

This book is also written for businesspeople who recognize that companies need to update their workplace rules. If they want to keep their best people they need to encourage love at work. If they don't do so promptly, unions are likely to seize these opportunities to attract new members.

WORKING YOUR WAY TO THE ALTAR

Don't select a job just to find a mate. Select a job that you're prepared to do and that you'll be happy with even after you've found the man of your choice.

DEVELOPING YOUR ACTION PLAN

Here you'll learn why love at work can work for you, how and where to look for eligible men, how to use your job to best advantage, what makes a job socially advantageous, and when you should change jobs to meet the man of your choice. You'll be able to examine sixty great jobs for meeting men and five that look great but are remarkably disappointing. We'll help you expand your horizons, to consider men who you might have overlooked before. Then you'll learn specific strategies for using your workplace to meet more and better men. You'll also learn how to start and develop a relationship while you're at work. Then you'll see how you can deal with your company and your co-workers, how to overcome obstacles to love at work, and how to avoid a relationship you don't want. Finally, we'll show you how to maximize your benefits from working with the man of your choice.

CHAPTER 1
Good News about Love at Work

You can have it all—your husband and your career. Best of all, you can find both in the same place—at work—if you know how and where to look. Start with your co-workers, then expand your horizons to your customers and clients as well as suppliers.

Love at work begins with friendship, develops into romance, and ultimately leads to marriage, bonding closely people who spend their days—and nights—together. Your camaraderie enhances both your job and your marriage. You'll have a closeness that few couples have, and your marriage will become more of a sharing experience. As love at work becomes more frequent, the divorce rate is likely to decline.

When you work together or in a related industry, you can understand each other's work environment in a way that an outsider can't. You can empathize with the other's competitive pressures, tight deadlines, emergencies, and other needs and problems. You can help each other in ways not possible in a conventional relationship.

Love at work can benefit your employer too, because you'll be happier and more productive at work and have greater company loyalty.

TIME IS OF THE ESSENCE

If you want love and marriage as well as career success, you can't waste time with conventional dating. Your most efficient and expedient way of husband-hunting, without diluting the effort you spend at work, is to look for love at work.

Figure out how little time you have for meeting men. If you're working and doing the chores to keep your life going, you'll have no more than two or three hours each weekday to call your own, and less if you also have school or family responsibilities. You might not even have these two or three hours as a single block of time, just an hour here and minutes there, so your activities outside of work provide few opportunities for meeting men. After a week of hard work, you might not have the energy to socialize and seek a suitable partner.

The only place where you spend enough time to meet and get to know a man is at work, so work becomes the natural place to meet men. In fact, you're more like your colleagues than members of your family, especially if you have many years of job training and work experience.

Many executive and professional women either marry colleagues or remain single. For a large number of career women, especially career women with children, there's no alternative to meeting men at work if they want marriage. They're too busy with family responsibilities and careers to become part of the singles scene. Your time and energy are not endless commodities. Since they are both expended at work, allocate a little of each to looking for an ideal mate.

You don't stop being a woman when you become an executive. You can have a successful career, as well as a husband and children, if you know how to use your time wisely. After all, a male doesn't stop being a man just because *he's* seeking career success.

ADVANTAGES TO LOVE AT WORK

Your Personal Benefits

1. You show your best personality at work—you're career-oriented and courageous.

2. You were hired because of your qualifications for your position. These qualifications can make you look good in a social context.

3. You're at your mental best, since you're using your talent, energy, and concentration on your job.

4. He won't say, "What's a nice girl like you doing in a place like this?"

5. The work environment gives you the chance to show the man you're intelligent and articulate, an opportunity rarely found at bars or parties.

6. You can be yourself to a much greater extent than you can in the singles scene.

7. You're well groomed and look good. You aren't wearing gobs of makeup, as you might if you were out "on the prowl." The less of a hunter you appear, the less threatening you are to men.

8. Business hours are active hours, enabling you to meet men while you're most alert.

9. You have a business purpose for starting a conversation with any man you want to meet.

10. Men can approach you easily by creating a business pretext.

11. Work-related social activities give you access to people you don't see daily.

12. You can use business and professional organizations to meet others in your field.

13. You're at work anyway. Proximity makes it relatively easy to meet people without wasting a great deal of energy or effort on the wrong person.

14. The men at work are your captive audience. Even if you don't make a great first impression, men can get to like you gradually over a period of time if they see you in the office on a regular basis.

15. You can meet in an atmosphere that's free from sexual pressure.

Observing Him

1. Frog kissing is minimized. He's faced competition for the job and won, so the company has done the first part of the weeding-out process for you. You'll quickly uncover the information you need to complete the process.

2. You'll find out his real priorities as he makes decisions and acts on them.

3. You can readily discover who is attracted to him and who he is attracted to.

4. Your co-workers will tell you what he is like, and you can observe him without his being aware you're watching.

5. He can act in a phony manner on a brief date, but not day in and day out at the office. You'll see him as he really is, so there will be fewer surprises, especially unpleasant ones. You'll see if he reacts the way you'd want your future husband to react. He'll look less glamorous initially, but more appealing over the long run.

Your Shortcut to Knowing Him

You can observe people more accurately at work than during artificial rituals called dates. Notice these ten facets of his personality at work because they carry over to romance:

1. Assertiveness

2. Capacity for stress, criticism, and boredom

3. Compassion

4. Generosity with money or time

5. Honesty

6. Patience

7. Self-esteem

8. Sense of humor

9. Stability (dedication to a project or idea)

10. Temper (how he deals with anger or bad moods)

Gathering Additional Information

The workplace gives you the opportunity to gather other information before you invest time in a relationship with him. Look at these ten characteristics:

1. Competence

2. Energy

3. Habits

4. Health

5. Intelligence

6. Lifestyle preferences

7. Manners

8. Sociability

9. Sophistication

10. Spending patterns

Mutual Benefits

1. You'll both know how much time you can spend together.

2. Your future plans will be more realistic. Realistic expectations lead to stronger relationships.

3. You'll have mutual friends and fewer social conflicts.

4. Relocation is easier if you both work for a company that can fill two job openings.

5. You can drive to work together, which continues the bonding while cutting your commuting costs. You might even be able to use the car pool lane.

ARE THE DISADVANTAGES REAL?

Opponents to love at work raise the following objections. Let's see how valid they really are.

Preoccupation

Some people claim that lovers who meet at work will become preoccupied with each other and with their relationship. However, this "rush" or extreme enthusiasm happens in all relationships, not just when you meet on your job or through your job. In fact, you're less likely to become preoccupied in the workplace because you may want to keep your relationship secret. You'll try to appear as no more than friends and colleagues and will try not to draw attention to yourselves. For this reason, you'll go to considerable effort to concentrate on your work.

Cover Up

Another potential objection to love at work is that lovers cover up each other's mistakes. Buddies do this too, so the romantic nature of the relationship is not the source of the problem. Sure, some mistakes may be covered up, but others may be corrected by the lover. Four eyes see better than two, two heads think better than one. Hopefully, your work environment will enable you to correct each other's mistakes rather than covering them up.

Lower Work Quality

Office romances are often accused of lowering work quality. It's true that romance sometimes reduces work quality initially because it takes priority over the job, but work quality then increases because neither lover has to take time away from work for mating purposes. Within a few weeks you should make up for any work you missed. You'll be helping each other succeed in your careers.

Influence

Some people object to love at work because they feel that the lovers will have too much influence on each other. Yet friendship and blood relationships also give one person influence over another. Also, influence is not necessarily a bad thing. Your influence on each other will be usually positive because you'll have your financial eggs in the same basket and care strongly about your mutual success.

Jealousy

Some people are afraid that love at work causes jealousy. They're right! People who don't have happy relationships of their own should be jealous. They would be upset over any advantage a co-worker had, whether it is a new desk, new love, or office with a window. Happy people enjoy seeing others happy. They feel a particular joy in seeing love at work. A number of people oppose love at work—until they find it themselves. Just wish them well.

Favoritism

Another objection is that one lover will show favoritism to the other. This problem is real, but it's most severe when the relationship is secret. If management is open to love at work, and knows about the relationship, it can then deal with any showing of favoritism. When you alone make a decision that favors your lover, be sure you back up this decision with solid facts and objective standards.

Loss of Confidentiality

Some people object to love at work because the lovers might tell each other things they normally wouldn't know. Sometimes it's necessary to keep secrets within an organization, but that's difficult to do when two people are lovers. You avoid this problem by working in activities where gathering and sharing information is encouraged.

Acquisition of Power

Another objection to love at work is that the two people will have more power together than they would have separately. This problem also arises when people have formed a bond because of their gender, ethnic background, schooling, or neighborhood. If you limit your contact with him at work and develop friendships with other workers, you'll dispel the argument that you are forming a power bloc.

CAN YOU FIND LOVE AT WORK?

Now that you're aware of the advantages to love at work, it's time to see if your job is enabling you to meet men you truly want. Take this quiz, for the result may surprise you. What you think is a great job may not be so great after all. You'll start thinking how you can change your job—perhaps slightly—to increase your opportunities for meeting men.

EVALUATING YOURSELF AND YOUR JOB

1. *How would you compare the number of men and number of women where you work?*
   (a) Men outnumber women by a ratio of more than 5 to 1

(b) Men outnumber women, but by less than 5 to 1
(c) There are more women than men

2. *The business is*
    (a) A large company (more than 1,000 employees)
    (b) A medium-size company (10–1,000 employees)
    (c) A small company (fewer than 10 employees)

3. *List all of the personal values you insist your future husband have (such as kindness, ambition, piety, and pride). How many values are on your list?*
    (a) 10 or fewer
    (b) 11 to 25
    (c) More than 25

4. *List your objective requirements for your future husband (such as height, weight, age, and intelligence). How many requirements do you have?*
    (a) 10 or fewer
    (b) 11 to 25
    (c) More than 25

5. *Compared with the education and work experience of your co-workers, yours is*
    (a) Less
    (b) About the same
    (c) Greater

6. *You generally network with women*
    (a) Who are directly in competition with you for men
    (b) Who have different taste in men
    (c) Very rarely; you generally mind your own business

7. *You can find out about people before you meet them*
    (a) Always
    (b) Sometimes
    (c) Never

8. *The color selection for your wardrobe could best be described as*
- (a) Subtle
- (b) Bright
- (c) Garish

9. *Can you shake hands with the people you encounter?*
- (a) Always
- (b) Sometimes
- (c) Never

10. *Your co-workers would describe you as*
- (a) Intimidating
- (b) Friendly
- (c) Timid

11. *Would you describe the job's excitement level as*
- (a) Extremely high
- (b) High
- (c) Low

12. *How physically clean would you be at work?*
- (a) "This is a clean job."
- (b) "It's usually rather clean."
- (c) "Everyone gets soiled and sweaty."

13. *How strenuous is the job?*
- (a) "It's very strenuous."
- (b) "It provides moderate exercise such as walking."
- (c) "It's totally sedentary."

14. *How stressful is the job?*
- (a) "It's stress-free."
- (b) "Sure, there's some stress, but..."
- (c) "There's a lot of stress here."

15. *Can you chat with others?*
- (a) Whenever you feel like it, as long as you get the work done

    (b) Every once in a while, on a break
    (c) Only once you leave work

16. *Can you use the phone at work?*
    (a) "Yes."
    (b) "Yes, but I can't speak privately."
    (c) "No."

17. *Would you describe the work travel as*
    (a) Extensive
    (b) Moderate
    (c) Minimal

18. *You work primarily with*
    (a) No one
    (b) Machines
    (c) Other people

19. *Who sets your work schedule?*
    (a) "My time is my own."
    (b) "My employer sets my schedule, but I usually know it in advance."
    (c) "I'm on call."

20. *What time do you leave work?*
    (a) Between 3 a.m. and 3 p.m.
    (b) Between 3 p.m. and 7 p.m.
    (c) Between 7 p.m. and 3 a.m.

21. *Does the employer attempt to control your off-work activities?*
    (a) Always
    (b) Sometimes
    (c) Never

22. *How many men do you meet each year?*
    (a) 10,000
    (b) 1,000
    (c) 100

23. *When you meet someone, the initial meeting lasts*
    (a) Under 5 minutes
    (b) 5 minutes to an hour
    (c) More than an hour

24. *How often do you see someone you meet through your job?*
    (a) Day in and day out
    (b) Three or five times during the year
    (c) Never again

25. *You are the only woman in a meeting. How many men are likely to be there?*
    (a) 1
    (b) 3
    (c) 30

26. *At work, how often can you meet privately with a man?*
    (a) Frequently
    (b) Rarely
    (c) Never

27. *Your encounters with men are predominantly*
    (a) Positive
    (b) Neutral
    (c) Negative

28. *Can you select the people you will be meeting?*
    (a) Always
    (b) Sometimes
    (c) Never

29. *Someone who meets you for the first time would conclude that you are*
    (a) Superficial
    (b) Significant
    (c) Nice, pleasant

30. *How many people who met you last year remember you now?*
- **(a)** Under 10
- **(b)** 10 to 100
- **(c)** Over 100

31. *How many people whom you met last year do you remember?*
- **(a)** Under 10
- **(b)** 10 to 100
- **(c)** Over 100

32. *Do you receive public recognition for your work?*
- **(a)** Never
- **(b)** Sometimes
- **(c)** Frequently

33. *What image does your job most closely portray?*
- **(a)** Kindness
- **(b)** Hard work
- **(c)** None

34. *Your job's status is*
- **(a)** High
- **(b)** Ordinary
- **(c)** Low

35. *Your business personality differs from your private personality*
- **(a)** By a wide margin
- **(b)** Somewhat
- **(c)** Very little

36. *When you're on the job, people are glad to see you*
- **(a)** Usually
- **(b)** Sometimes
- **(c)** Never

37. *Your job gives you access to information about eligible men*
   (a) Frequently
   (b) Sometimes
   (c) Never

38. *You can control your work encounters*
   (a) Usually
   (b) Sometimes
   (c) Rarely

39. *Your compensation, compared with that of others, is*
   (a) High
   (b) Average
   (c) Low

40. *You can claim a tax deduction for taking a man to dinner*
   (a) Sometimes
   (b) Rarely
   (c) Never

EVALUATING YOUR ANSWERS

Questions	Answers	Questions	Answers
1	b	21	c
2	b	22	b
3	a	23	b
4	a	24	b
5	c	25	b
6	b	26	a
7	a	27	a
8	b	28	a
9	a	29	b
10	b	30	c
11	b	31	c
12	a	32	c
13	b	33	a
14	b	34	a
15	a	35	c
16	a	36	a
17	b	37	a
18	c	38	a
19	a	39	a
20	b	40	a

Now tally up your responses to determine how your job rates:

36–40 You have great opportunities for finding love at work.

31–35 You can find love at work with some effort.

26–30 You may need to restructure your job or your personal life to find love at work.

21–25 You may need to restructure both your job and your personal life to have any hope of finding love at work.

0–20 Have you considered celibacy?

CHAPTER 2

Using Your Job
to Meet Men

Your job should be fulfilling to you, but this may require a
social dimension, an opportunity to meet eligible men. For
some of you, this may be one of the more important
considerations in your job selection. "Meetability" may affect your choice of career, and once you've chosen your
career, it may affect your choice of employer. It may also
affect your choice of location, your work hours, and your
specific job-function. In this chapter we'll look at the forty
crucial criteria you can use to evaluate your present job, or
any potential job, in terms of the opportunities it provides
for meeting men.

THE MEN YOU CAN MEET

If you're looking for love at work, consider how many
men you'll be in contact with on the job and how many of
them meet your list of expectations. You should also be
thinking about the ratio of men to women, business size,
quality and availability of the men, competition from other
women, and opportunities for networking.

Too Many Women, Too Few Men

You're looking to meet more and better men, but *more* doesn't necessarily mean *better.* The number of men does make a difference, and so does the ratio of men to women.

The relative number of men and women affects your chances of meeting the man of your choice, but be careful not to overemphasize this ratio. It's just one consideration among many in determining if a particular career or a specific job provides enough significant opportunities for meeting eligible men.

Also, don't assume that a higher male–female ratio means better opportunities when it comes to meeting men. When this ratio is too high, the men might view their job as an all-male preserve and might resent your presence. Besides, you'd be too visible, and your actions would receive such great scrutiny that it would be difficult to meet men. A man would be afraid to ask you out because his buddies would never let him live it down if you rejected him. You'd have to overcome this disadvantage by being aggressive and approaching the man you want, but you may not feel comfortable being that aggressive.

If you take a job that has been all male, you'll be advancing the cause of women's rights, but not increasing your chances of dating and mating. Choose a career where the male–female ratio is less extreme, such as law or medicine.

If there are many more women than men where you work, there's too much competition for male attention. If a man meets hundreds of women, you'll have to be spectacular to be noticed above the rest. Instead of trying and failing, you'll do better by looking elsewhere.

An ideal male–female ratio is as low as 1 to 1 or as high as 5 to 1. If the ratio is lower where you work, you'll have too much competition. If it's higher, you'll be too noticeable for your own good.

Business Size

The best opportunities for meeting men aren't found in giant corporations or small businesses, but in medium-size companies.

A medium-size company is large enough to give you broader responsibilities, enabling you to mingle with co-workers in other departments. Your networking possibilities are more diverse than if you work for an industrial giant where you're limited to one area.

Medium-size companies are often small enough to have a family spirit. Everyone is welcome to participate in social events. If the company is small enough that it uses outside accounting, advertising, legal, and maintenance services, you'll have more opportunities to meet the many outsiders who constantly pass through.

In a giant company you'll meet more people on the job, while in a medium-size company you'll meet more people through the job.

Meeting Your Needs

"All men are created equal" is one of our fundamental beliefs—but it need not be part of your dating strategy. All men may benefit from the Gettsyburg Address, but they shouldn't have access to yours. You can—and should—be selective and judge men as potential mates, but don't eliminate men at first glance unless they're just awful. At this point, start with the man's basic subjective values, goals, and interests to see if they match yours.

You may think your criteria for a husband are reasonable and realistic, but your ideal mate may be scarcer than one in a billion if you treat each item on your wish list as a basic requirement. Narrow your requirements to no more than ten (such as attitude toward family, attitude toward sex, attitude toward money, political beliefs, career goals, place where you would like to live, and lifestyle expectations). If you have as many as ten independent criteria and half the men satisfy each one, your ideal mate will still be scarcer than one in a thousand, so try to narrow your requirements even further.

Once you establish your own requirements, you'll discover that men in some jobs are far more likely to meet these requirements than men in other jobs. These other men may be fine for someone else, but not you.

Very often, a man's personality is a crucial factor in the career he chooses. If you want a man who is the milk of human kindness, look for him in social work or school teaching. He probably won't be a movie producer, lawyer, or newspaper editor.

If you're sensitive about what is prim and proper and would be embarrassed to keep a bowling ball in your living room or have a non-pedigreed pooch as a pet, try to avoid engineers. They don't enjoy conforming for the sake of appearances and are much more interested in substance than in form. So what if the four burners of the stove don't match. They work, and that's what matters.

Here are some further generalizations that you might find useful:

- Accountants and bankers are more frugal than salesmen and advertising executives. Just ask waitresses about tipping patterns.

- Executives are more willing to relocate than are professional people. They don't have to pass burdensome exams each time they move.

- Employees are more likely than entrepreneurs to seek early retirement. Some people find running a business more fun than golf or tennis.

People have different priorities, so there will be trade-offs, but beware of conflicting criteria. It's difficult to find a man who is generous but who also knows the value of money, because if he does, he expects to keep his hard-earned bucks.

Once you establish your own personal criteria, evaluate

the type of men drawn to that occupation. This is difficult to do if you're an outsider, but the difficulty does not diminish its importance. At this point, you'll be evaluating a group of men rather than an individual man. That comes later. Of course, you can find a lime in a bin full of lemons, but it's easier to find a lime in the lime bin. Go where there's a high possibility of finding men who meet your requirements.

Who's Eligible?

How available are the men you are meeting on your present job, or where you might consider working? Even if you think every man is available, you'd have to admit that some men are more available than others, and that some jobs won't help your cause.

What information do you need to determine how many men in the company are truly eligible and available to you? You probably have some basic objective requirements such as age, marital status, physical condition, mental condition, race, and religion. Whatever your requirements, find out how many men meet them. Even if you don't care about a particular factor, recognize that each man you meet has his own requirements and might rule you out as his potential mate.

You don't want to waste your emotions and time, so ask him as soon as the opportunity arises about his ideal mate, the lifestyle he desires, and his attitudes about issues that matter to you. Use stories from your newspaper to get his views instead of asking him directly so you don't appear overly interested in him.

Competition

You've been finding out a great deal about the men, but you also need to learn the crucial facts about the women, especially those who are looking for men. Then compare your emotional, mental, and physical attributes with theirs. Education and experience are both plusses, but so is youth.

If both the women and the men are significantly younger and better educated than you are, your marriage prospects will diminish. Summer camp may be a great place to work when you're eighteen, but a lousy place to work when you're forty-eight.

Networking

Some information you need about the men in the company is not easy to find. And you're not even looking for the low-down on specific men yet, just the basic demographic data about the quality, quantity, and availability of men on the job.

The facts you're trying to uncover are not published in a company's annual report. Conventional placement counselors and employment agencies don't have this information either.

Where can you turn? Your most effective strategy is to network with the other single women who are seeking marriage. If you're going to work for the first time, or are looking to change jobs, you may already know women who work for the company you're considering.

In your quest for your ideal mate, you'll have to be competitive with other women, just as you are competitive with both men and women in your pursuit of career opportunities. Nevertheless, networking and bonding can be mutually advantageous, especially if you network in a thoughtful manner with women who share your goals but aren't directly in competition with you.

WORK ENVIRONMENT

Your physical work environment, whether it is the executive office suite, the restaurant counter, or the lathe, has a major impact on *your* meetability. You're going to look very different to a man if you're behind a desk, in a toll booth, or next to an assembly line.

The less you interface with machines and products, and the more you interface with people, the greater your meetability—assuming you are looking for a man, not a machine!

These fifteen factors are key facets of your work environment. Take them into account if you're selecting a job in which you can meet men for marriage, or when you think about ways to improve your present situation. You won't have everything in your favor, but try to avoid a job replete with disadvantages.

1. Preview Power

Can you find out about people before you meet them? If so, you have the opportunity to be more selective and eliminate those you find clearly unattractive. Of course, if the other person can find out about you before meeting, you may be the one who's eliminated. Here are three jobs that can give you this preview advantage:

- Portrait painter—you'll see his photo before you decide to do his portrait.

- Investigator—are you going to look for him or let him remain among the missing?

- Executive recruiter—you'll see his photo and employment record, which may influence how closely you'd care to work with him.

2. Visibility

Some people are more visible than others. The more distinct you are, the more visible you are. Women in business and the professions are usually more visible than their male counterparts because they're fewer in number.

Visibility is a plus, but within limits. If you're too visible, you lose your freedom of action. Celebrities are often so visible that they're never really in private, which makes it harder for them to start a relationship. Since that is not your problem, increase your visibility. Participate actively in meetings, say hello to everyone at work, and walk proudly. Make sure your wardrobe is bright rather than subtle, but don't look garish either. When it comes to job selection, be sure to choose one that gives you the opportunity to be visible, not hidden.

3. Physical Barriers

Physical barriers make it difficult to meet men because they impede contact and intimidate people on at least one side of the barrier. These are a few commonplace jobs that have physical barriers:

- Token clerk in a subway booth
- Prison guard
- Bank teller behind the security window
- Shop clerk behind the counter
- Armored car driver

If you can't shake hands with the people you encounter, the physical barrier is severe. But even an executive who sits at a desk has a barrier—the desk itself. The bigger the desk, the bigger the barrier.

If your job has physical barriers, use the off-duty time to meet men. Stand at a window that has an outside view for a few minutes before you start work, or sit outside on a bench for part of your lunch hour. Be accessible to others so they can have a few minutes privacy to talk with you.

If you can't remove the physical barriers where you work, you may need to transfer to another job if you're serious about looking for love. If you're a plant administrator who's behind a desk, consider becoming a shop foreman or union steward. If you're the assistant marketing manager, you may do better as the director of new business development. If you're the shop clerk who is trapped behind the counter, change to a department where you can go out on the selling floor.

4. Psychological Barriers

Psychological barriers impede access in much the same way as physical barriers. Your job may have no barbed wire or fence posts, but its accoutrements may intimidate men. These psychological barriers may be as small as an expensive pen, your briefcase, or your power suit. A sophisticated calculator, erudite treatise, or gold braid on your uniform are additional barriers.

Overcome psychological barriers by starting conversations with those whom you encounter at work. Assure your co-workers and clients they'll at least get the courtesies of the day from you. Start with the friendly hello, but don't expect a romantic greeting until you know each other well.

Minimize psychological barriers if you can do so without diminishing your business stature. Get rid of the diamond stick pin and gold watch. But if you must choose, retain your business image and use other ways to reduce the intimidation factor.

5. Job Stimuli

Is your work stimulating, giving you "food for thought," or dull and boring, merely giving you "thought for food"? If your job provides you with a full measure of stimuli that create emotional impacts, you'll become a much more exciting person in your social life. Here are jobs that provide many sensory inputs: talk show host, fashion designer, magazine editor, and political leader.

Yet too many sensory inputs can interfere with your

relationships, especially if you are an air traffic controller, police officer, or firefighter. Look for a job with many sensory inputs, but not that many. If your job is too stimulating, you'll need a few hours of unwinding before socializing.

6. *Job Cleanliness*

The cleanliness of your job affects your appeal while at work. Some jobs don't let you appear spotless no matter how personally clean you are. If you're a butcher, a baker, or candlestick maker, your outfit or hands are likely to get soiled during work. The gardener and the household worker are not physically clean at work, nor is the worker in heavy industry. The cook and the athlete also face this problem, especially if they perspire heavily. A woman who is a painter or a chemist is in a similar situation. If, like a surgeon, you can change your soiled clothing before meeting the public, you can solve this problem.

If you're not physically clean at work, but you want to meet someone through your job, rather than someone who works with you, you'll need to change jobs.

7. *Strenuousness*

Take a look at your physical energy level and the energy that the job requires. A strenuous job leaves you less energy for dating and mating. If you're exhausted, you're not much fun to be with. If you're seeking an active social life, don't take a job that requires too much of your energy.

Are you on your feet all day? Are you carrying trays? Are you squinting at a computer screen? Or peering through a microscope? Eyestrain and muscle strain take their toll. Sore feet and calluses on your hands also diminish your availability for dating. Don't confuse exercise with strain, or use with abuse. A job that abuses you physically causes even worse problems than hindering your social life. If you are a police officer, firefighter, steelworker, or waitress, your job is so strenuous that your social life is likely to suffer.

Jobs that provide some exercise, such as walking, can help your social life. If you're a manufacturer's representative calling on downtown customers, you'll benefit socially from walking from one office to another.

8. Stress

Stress at work can affect your activities after work. Your job's stress level can affect your overall ability to relate to others and have fun, and even your opportunities to date successfully.

The fact that stress affects dating does not mean that stress should be avoided. Contrary to what you may have read, the least stressful job isn't the best, at least when it comes to your dating plans. Too much stress is a clear disadvantage because it saps the mental and emotional energies you'll need for dating and mating and may lead to alcohol abuse or drug dependency. Inadequate stress is disadvantageous too, as it can cause boredom. You need some stress to get the adrenaline flowing.

A job that is stressful for one person is not necessarily stressful for another. Look at your own stress level and determine your stress tolerance. You know how much you can tolerate before you feel mentally or emotionally drained. Stress usually comes from deviating from your natural self, or because job demands don't match your likes or abilities. The more you try to change your personality or force yourself, the higher the stress level.

The cloistered nun may have lowest stress level, but that occupation certainly does not lead to an active social life. The air traffic controller has a very high level of stress, which weakens the controller's ability to function in a social context. Jobs with a moderate stress level, such as salesperson, lawyer, or hairstylist, create the best mental atmosphere for meeting people.

9. *Opportunities for Personal Conversation*

You almost always have some chance to speak with your co-workers, but you may not have the chance to speak with outsiders. Jobs that give you the opportunity to chat with suppliers or customers are clearly preferable. Most office occupations give you the chance to have personal conversations with outsiders. Sales occupations provide similar benefits, but most factory jobs and repetitive service occupations don't. In many jobs, such as an order taker in a fast food restaurant, business conversations tend to be brief, and personal conversations are largely precluded. Avoid these jobs if you can.

Personal conversations among co-workers are one of the best ways to meet the man of your choice. Most offices have a lunch room or employees' lounge or someplace where employees can socialize on their breaks.

Initiate contact through a brief social chat, just long enough to find out one bit of personal information. Upon meeting, you won't be asking "Do you like me?" or "Are you married?" Save these questions until later. But you can ask "Where are you going for vacation this year"? "Did you enjoy the long weekend?" Then you can start exchanging more personal information.

10. *Telephone Availability*

Telephone access is an important facet of dating. Your work-time conversations with someone you date might be brief and infrequent, but you should be able to reach him and he should be able to reach you. If you can't get to a phone and call him, you may lose out in the competitive struggle to find a mate. If he can't reach you by phone, you may be even worse off.

The man should be able to call you during the day to plan dates, to find out more about you, and to reveal his inner thoughts to you. When he's excited about good news and you're the first person he can share it with, that sharing bonds you closer together.

You should have your own phone at work and be able to talk privately, but some jobs give you limited phone access or let others overhear. Other jobs, like being an outside sales representative, take you away from the phone for extended time periods. People hate to call back repeatedly. If you're not there, both of you lose out. Consider a car phone if you spend time in the car and can afford one. An answering machine helps if it takes your messages and lets you call in for them, but it's not the same as reaching *you.* An answering service is usually better than a machine, especially if callers will receive a personalized message in response when they call.

11. Travel on the Job

Your travels can help—or hinder—your chances to meet and marry your ideal mate. Travel increases your chances of meeting more people and enhances your courage to say hello to strangers. It also provides important sensory inputs that can make you a more interesting conversationalist and a better companion. Yet too much travel makes it hard to start and maintain a relationship.

Travel on the job can become repetitious, and no more fun than commuting. You might not be traveling to the most exciting places, but even if you are, the most exciting locale can get boring if you're alone.

Some job travel can enhance your relationship, especially if you can bring the one you love with you. Before you accept a job, discover your employer's attitudes toward your traveling with another person.

Too much travel can harm a relationship or prevent one from developing fully, because travel can break the continuity and the bonding. Without contact, relationships wither and die. If your job requires you to be away from the one you love for more than a week at a time, travel is adversely

affecting your relationship. Even short but frequent trips can
be disadvantageous.

The travels of a pilot or cabin attendant seem glamorous, but these folks complain about how difficult it is to
sustain a relationship. Usually, they end up going out with
other crew members. If you must travel frequently, go to the
same hotels and restaurants and network with people you
travel with and those you meet there.

12. Work Station

Are you working in a "bullpen" with dozens of other
office workers, on a shop floor, or behind a restaurant counter? If so, you lack personal privacy. This lack of privacy has
both positive and negative effects when it comes to meeting
people.

You don't need your own office. In fact, you may be
better off without it, but office sharing is often the worst of
both worlds. In sharing, your activities become obvious to
your suitemates, yet you're isolated from everyone else. In
the bullpen, it's easy to say hello and start a conversation. If
you're friendly with those who work nearby, you'll develop
some signal that you need a few minutes of privacy. If not,
offer to walk back with him to his desk as if you were just
heading in that direction.

It's difficult enough for a man to approach you when
you're alone and start a conversation or ask you out. If
others around you can possibly see you reject him, it's even
harder for him to approach. Try to find a private place
where a brief conversation won't be heard by others.

13. Work Schedule

Can you choose when you work? When it comes to
meeting and marrying the man of your choice, a job in
which your time is your own is preferable to one with a

rigid schedule. It's easier to have a flexible work schedule if you're your own boss or if you are an outside salesperson.

If you have to break dates often because of your job, your fellow might convince himself you're avoiding him or playing with his emotions. Minimize this risk by showing him your official schedule so he knows you're not avoiding him. Insist on a rain check to indicate you really enjoy spending time with him.

14. Working Hours

The time of day at which you meet someone can affect the value of the encounter from a dating standpoint. Encounters that are too early in the day lose some of their value because there's work to get done and schedules to keep. Encounters that are later than the normal dating time can also be disadvantageous because most folks are exhausted by then. When you're off work, try to meet men during the late afternoon or early evening since you're not on a tight schedule and these hours are conducive to relaxing. This is a great time to meet your colleagues who work for other companies.

Your response to someone is affected by the time when you meet the person. You have attitudes and prejudices concerning time and are likely to view someone you meet at 7 p.m. more favorably than someone you meet at 3 a.m. Also, your energy level and attitude are affected by time. Be alert to your body clock and to the way others in society react to you at different times of the day.

Select a job with good working hours from a social standpoint. You should be leaving work between 3 p.m. and 7 p.m. so you can meet people when you and they are both receptive. If you work odd hours, become familiar with the restaurants, laundromats, supermarkets, gas stations, drug stores, and hangouts that are open on your schedule.

15. *Personal Freedom*

Can your employer dictate your life patterns when you're off work? If so, you lose a great deal of personal freedom. You also lose personal freedom if you bring the job home with you, such as in police work, the clergy, the military, and medicine.

An employer might try to dictate your personal life even when you're not in one of these occupations. Your employer can legitimately make sure you don't engage in activities contrary to your organization's goals, but has no right to influence your life beyond that point.

A company's work environment, especially its employment policies, can greatly influence your opportunities to find love at work. These are some questions you should be able to answer: Does the employer follow a policy forbidding or restricting your personal dating lives? Does the company seek employees who are unattached, available to travel or work odd hours? Are the first years so demanding on an employee that social life is minimal?

Here's a way to see how much your job restricts your personal freedoms: Can you pose for a girlie magazine without getting fired? Can you live with a man? Must you join certain organizations? Must you contribute to a certain political party? Can you avoid giving to the company-backed charity? Dating is just one of the ways in which you'll be putting this personal freedom to use. Select a job that maximizes your personal freedom or live far from the job to avoid scrutiny.

MAKING CONTACT

If you're looking for love at work, the *way* you meet people and the encounters you have are as important as the nature of your job, the people you meet, and the impression you make.

When you are evaluating a job in terms of its "encounter

potential," there are ten facets of the encounters you should consider.

1. Number

If you are asked "How many men do you want to meet?" you might reply "The more the better." But, in reality, you could meet *too* many men and not have the chance to get to know them well enough to identify which ones might be potential mates.

You're better off meeting a few men each day than meeting a few dozen men each day. You can be memorable to a few men, and they're likely to remember you unless they're meeting large numbers of women, but it's unrealistic to expect dozens of men who meet you briefly really remember you.

Ideally, your goal should be to meet a thousand men each year. One hundred is too few and ten thousand is too many. You should be meeting three or four men each day. That's all you need to meet a thousand men each year.

2. Duration

Encounters provide maximum benefit if they are between five minutes and two hours in length.

Very short encounters provide virtually no opportunity to get to know the other person. These contacts are essentially valueless from the standpoint of dating and mating. The ticket taker at an amusement park or movie theater or the seller of subway tokens has contact that lasts a fraction of a second. They *encounter* thousands of men but meet no one.

Your encounter with a man must last long enough for you to be memorable. You need at least a few minutes for him to find out your name and tell you his, to relate a few incidents, and to indicate friendliness and interest in meeting again. Encounters that are longer than an hour are generally disadvantageous because boredom sets in, especially if you must keep the conversation at your workplace impersonal.

Also, if your encounters are long, you lose the chance to meet others. Your goal should be to learn enough facts about the man so that if you're interested in him you could say, "I've enjoyed our brief conversation. You're unusually interesting and I hope that soon we'll have the chance to talk again." If he is interested in you, that will be enough for him to act.

3. Frequency and Repetition

Would you prefer a job in which you never see the same person twice, or a job in which you keep seeing the same people over and over again? The middle ground is the best place to be, where you have some degree of repeat contact with the people you meet, but you don't see the same people day in and day out.

Unless you're particularly unique, like a movie star, you'll need a number of encounters to make a lasting impression in someone's mind. Otherwise, you won't be remembered. The number of encounters you need varies from person to person, but somewhere between three and five encounters should register you on his mind.

4. Exclusivity of Encounters

You're more memorable when no other women are present. If everyone else is male, you're certain to stand out. When other women are present, you're competing with these other women, at least to some extent, for male attention.

However, if the group is too large, exclusivity ceases to work in your favor. You become too visible and too subject to scrutiny.

If there are thirty men in the meeting, and you're the only woman, you'll be a topic of conversation. Each man will figure he has only a one in thirty chance of impressing you. With these odds, he won't try, especially if he doesn't know the competition and can't evaluate his chances of surpassing the odds. Adding a few other women will normalize the encounter. You want to stand out, but not too far.

You'll do better if you're the only woman and are meeting three men. In competing with two others, each man still can feel enough confidence to seek your attention. Even if a man doesn't ask you out directly, he'll look for clues as to which one you favor and the probability of his success. These clues include a longer look, bigger smile, and a comment that you hope to see him again.

5. Privacy

Meeting someone privately has real advantages once physical safety is no longer a concern, and the work environment provides many good reasons to see someone without making romantic motivations obvious. When your encounters are private, he is far more likely to open up and talk about himself honestly. If other men are present, he won't reveal any weaknesses about himself, even about his past indiscretions. In fact, he may go on a boasting spree in front of other men.

Also, if you are looking to impress a particular man, but not his colleagues, meeting alone lets you focus all your attention on him and ask personal questions.

6. Positiveness

It's great to have positive encounters, but it isn't essential. It's more important to be memorable. You can turn a negative initial encounter into a positive relationship if you can see the other person again, but you can't turn indifference into anything.

If you're meeting men on your job or through your job, there are two ways to make the meeting upbeat: the positiveness that your company's product or service evokes, and the personal positiveness that you create.

Of course, some jobs evoke negative feelings. Here your goal should be to isolate the negative feelings toward the job and separate these feelings from the positive attitudes he might have toward you as a person. This is especially important if you are a dentist, tax auditor, or highway patrol officer.

Even working in the complaint department gives you the opportunity to meet men. A man comes in fighting mad and vents his hostility and anger while you solve his problems. But his anger could turn to relief and even affection for you, especially if you tell him that he's "too special a person to be treated in any manner except with the greatest consideration."

7. Choice of Encounters

A job in which you can choose whom you're going to meet is a tremendous plus for your social life. Do you go to different places when you're working or do you stay put and have people come to you? The more mobility you have, the more control you have over whom you meet. If you can meet only the men who come in through the door, or if you can meet only the men who are on the schedule your boss has set up for you, that's limiting.

The greater your ability to choose whom you meet, the better the job from a dating standpoint. You're far more likely to have this freedom of choice if you're an independent businessperson or salesperson rather than a factory worker or office employee.

8. Quality of the Encounter

Substantial encounters are better than superficial ones. Both your personality and your job can make an encounter substantial but you don't need a high-level job to have a quality encounter.

To be taken seriously by the men you meet, use your appearance, vocabulary, and demeanor to show that you're a woman of substance.

9. Intensity of Contact

A man can't follow up on an initial contact if he doesn't remember you. Intense encounters make people memorable. It's more important that an encounter be intense than it is for the encounter to be pleasant. What creates intensity? Power, surprise, or anticipation. People who meet in automobile accidents sometimes marry each other. Intensity is that important.

Make being memorable a primary goal of any contact you have with men. Think of the large number of people you encountered this week, or even yesterday. Chances are, you remember very few of the people you meet. Don't be surprised if very few people you meet remember you unless you make yourself memorable.

If an encounter is particularly intense, you certainly will be remembered. Some occupations lead to intense encounters. If you're a police officer or part of the fire-rescue service, you can make a profound impact on many of the people you meet. That's a good beginning to a relationship. When you help someone through a crisis, you're a friend forever.

10. Memory

The key to any encounter is remembering the person you meet. If you don't, you'll have no impetus for following up. Even if you meet a thousand men each year, you might remember just a few. If so, consider learning techniques that will help you improve your memory.

Jobs that give you the opportunity to build a file on the

men or compile a dossier help you remember the men you meet. Some jobs make the people you meet memorable, while some make you memorable to them. A few jobs, such as executive recruiter and loan officer, do both.

MAKING AN IMPRESSION

When you meet someone on your job or through your job, there are many facets of the impression you make, including your appearance, the attitude conveyed by the job, and the way in which others respond to you. Since your first impression may be your last or may be lasting, you want this impression to be strong and favorable.

1. Public Recognition

If you receive any awards or public recognition in connection with your job, you're increasing your opportunities to meet eligible men. You'll benefit whether you receive the Nobel Prize for Medicine or a restaurant's employee-of-the-month award. Your colleagues may congratulate you at the ceremony or send you a note later, but you've made a strong positive impression and have given them a business excuse for pursuing you. Many companies have initiated awards programs so that salespeople, hotel workers, and people in other occupations now receive recognition.

2. Image

A job may create an image. Some jobs portray power while others reflect kindness. But a large number of jobs portray no image at all. A job that conveys a good image increases your appeal. An image that is sharp but negative is preferable to one that is neutral and blurry.

A blue or dark brown uniform creates an image of

power, but a white uniform needs accoutrements to convey a power image. Military and police uniforms convey power. While you're wearing one of these uniforms, you'll appear to be a no-nonsense type of person. It's little wonder that security guards wear police-type uniforms.

Some uniforms, especially uniforms that are clean and white, convey kindliness and helpfulness. Nurses, physicians, and other medical personnel have an advantage here because their uniforms evoke a pleasant response from most people.

What image does your job convey? Is friendliness associated with your position? Does it have an intellectual aura? Does a uniform reveal your authority? Does your job provide major decision-making power that makes your position intimidating?

If your job's image is a negative one, you may be able to overcome that image, but it isn't easy to do so. Just think about the many actors who played a particular character and never were able to shake that image. Counteract a negative image by associating yourself with an upbeat organization or cause.

3. Job Status

High job status is attractive and intimidating at the same time. Since you can overcome this intimidation with friendliness, job status can be used to your social advantage.

If you view your occupation with pride, and others do too, you'll have a real advantage in meeting men. It's important that the man feel proud of what you do and that his family and others who influence his judgment will respond in an approving manner when he tells them what you do for a living. Of course, you don't know how a specific man will react before you know something about him, but you do know how society as a whole views your occupation.

Some women still take jobs that have lower status than the jobs for which they are qualified in the hope that this will help them meet men. Don't make this mistake. The increased self-esteem you get from a higher-level job will make you more desirable to men. If you can't take pride in your job, then take pride in striving for a better one.

4. Personality

Few of us go to work "as is." We change our physical appearance and our mental attitudes. Getting ready for work takes effort, but this effort is compounded if it must be continued on the job. The more your job personality deviates from your private personality, the greater effort you must expend to maintain your public personality at work.

If it takes effort for you to maintain a businesslike personality, you are better off with a job that requires fewer adjustments. To the extent that you can be the real you, men will be able to appreciate you as you really are.

5. Receptivity

Are people really glad to see you? They won't be if your opening line is "I'm the tax collector and I'm here to help you" or "I'm the undertaker who will be removing the corpse" or "I have a warrant to search the premises." Many jobs that have negative connotations usually give you tremendous access to people. Who has more access to the public than a politician?

When people have negative feelings about your job, they may (and probably do) hold these feelings against you on a personal level, at least at the outset. There are trade-offs, because some of these jobs also provide easy access and a few provide a pleasant physical image (like a physician's garb), but the job's receptivity may be more important to you. People will become more receptive if you display empathy toward them by your tone of voice, patience, or concern for their physical comfort.

MONEY AND POWER

Information, money, and power have an important role in the dating context as they do in other facets of life. A job that provides you with information about men you would like to meet, power to select some encounters and avoid others, and money to use in conjunction with dating is better than a job that doesn't offer you these opportunities.

1. Access to Information

Some jobs give you access to a great deal of information about the men you work with. You may be able to find out whether he's really divorced or just living apart from his wife, whether he's filed for bankruptcy, or whether he's suffering from prolonged impotence.

Jobs that give you access to inside information include positions in personnel, payroll, and medical departments. You might also get this information if you are an auditor or work for top management. Companies can't keep their confidential information 100 percent private, so you might as well be the beneficiary.

2. Control of the Situation

Control is an important asset in the dating context, just as it is in the business context. If you have a significant measure of control over potential and actual relationships, you can determine the direction of communication and the timing of encounters, and at least to some extent, select the people around you.

The ticket taker has no flexibility in conversation, but the executive has a great deal of flexibility. Many jobs will give you this control, even though they are not at an executive level.

3. Money

Yes, dating does take money. Even if your goals in life do not include getting rich, your earnings affect your "datability." You'll need money for your home and car as well as for your wardrobe and entertaining. You're probably bearing some of the dating expenses, too. Earning power is certainly relevant from a dating standpoint unless Grandpa left you a fortune or your former husband turned over his car, the one that now bears the license plate "Was His." Money won't buy you a honey, but major bills and poverty sure can scare off a man.

4. Tax Considerations

You have an advantage if you can treat your dinner companion as a prospective customer for your computer software or a client for your law firm as well as a potential mate. You may have the chance to deduct some of these expenses when you figure your taxes. A man may feel more comfortable about accepting your invitation if your employer or the government is paying for the date.

CHAPTER 3

Choosing and Changing Jobs

You can succeed at a large number of careers, and with many different companies. Why not choose a career and company in which you can meet the man of your choice? Pick your job wisely from a social standpoint as well as a financial one.

OCCUPATIONS THAT HELP YOU MEET MEN

Let's look at four categories of occupations, based on the way in which each gives you access to men, so you can determine the category that's most appropriate for you. All four categories give the opportunity to meet men through your job, while the third category also gives you many opportunities to meet men on the job.

Nurturing

Nurturing occupations provide a man with care or comfort. These are the traditionally female jobs, such as the nurse, stewardess, or waitress. The traditional nurturing occupations have one great advantage—the man's guard is usually down, so it's easier to get to know him once you meet. However, these jobs are relatively low-paying and require considerable physical stamina. Also, the large number of women in these fields increases competition for eligible men.

Power

The second category provides you with power, which gives you easy access to men. Occupations in this group include police officer, tax assessor, and security guard. These occupations help you meet men you wouldn't normally encounter, but you meet them under adverse circumstances when their guard is up. These occupations are useful for meeting men only if you can turn the men's antagonism into affection.

Male Predominance

This group includes careers in which most of the participants are male. You may be outnumbered by a wide margin, but you can meet your colleagues and choose from among the best. These occupations include traditionally male-dominated fields such as medicine, law, engineering, horse racing, and stock car racing. Each requires considerable effort and training, and there are easier ways to meet men, so undertake one of these occupations primarily for career fulfillment, not to find a husband.

Job Interaction

These jobs give you access to men who are your customers, suppliers, or clients. The category includes yacht service, automobile sales, computer repair, medical equipment sales, sports uniform cleaning, or tax return preparation. You can also meet a man by being his bank officer or investment adviser, or by selling him ties or shoes, or by being his hairstylist. If you're part of the media, you can interview men from various walks of life. These jobs enable you to meet segments of the public that are predominantly male. In almost all cases, this fourth category of occupations gives you the greatest opportunities to meet men, meeting men through your job.

HAVING IT ALL

Finding love at work is only one of your goals in job hunting. To interrelate this goal with your quest for money, power, stability, and your other work-related goals, it's helpful to categorize jobs by their primary characteristics:

1. *Talent*—music, art, sports, acting, inventor, entrepreneur, explorer, writer

2. *Brains*—law, medicine, accounting, university professor, scientist

3. *Skill*—plumber, carpenter, jeweler, optometrist, medical technician

4. *Effort*—truck driver, taxi driver

5. *Consistency*—toll booth collector, factory worker, security guard

Career opportunities at the top of this list are usually among the best for meeting men. You get a double benefit from developing your talents and using your brains—higher status and a better social life.

Where talent is the key, the person usually has high compensation and prestige, as well as a strong sense of uniqueness. Brains come next since professionals are usually highly regarded and highly compensated. Skilled workers are third, followed by unskilled but hardworking individuals, and then by the rest of the workforce. This sequence of talent—

brains—skill—effort—consistency—differs relatively little from one part of the world to the other, and (except for the treatment of entrepreneurial skill) is generally applicable regardless of the country's economic level or political system.

TARGETING YOUR MAN

You may really want a man who has a certain career. Don't be ashamed of these thoughts. Even if you have a successful business or a high-powered profession of your own, your future husband's career may be important to you. Why not target the man you really want?

If marriage, not your career, is your personal priority, you may be more willing to adjust your job plans. If you're looking for a man who has a specific occupation, choose your job accordingly.

Now that women are advancing in their careers, men are targeting them because of their professional attributes as well as their sexual attributes. Men want a woman who is brilliant and beautiful, with a successful career of her own. Often their ideal woman is a newscaster or talk show host, not a waitress or grocery clerk. Men are targeting the women they want, so don't be reluctant to do your own targeting.

When a woman does choose a man by his career, these are ten of the most popular choices:

Athlete	Entrepreneur
Clergyman	Lawyer
Corporate executive	Newscaster
Elected official	Physician
Engineer	Professor

Let's look at the best careers for meeting each of these men.

Athlete
Agent
Athlete
Business manager
Equipment manager
Journalist

Newscaster
Orthopedic physician
Tax adviser
Umpire/referee
Uniform designer

Clergyman
Deacon
Editor of church
  bulletin
Fundraiser
Lawyer
Minister

Organist
Salesperson,
  religious books
Secretary
Social worker
Usher

Corporate Executive
Accountant
Advertising account
  manager
Banker
Computer specialist
Corporate executive

Employee relations
  consultant
Financier
Lawyer
Pension specialist
Travel specialist

Elected Official
Bodyguard
Business executive
Civic leader
Elected official
Lawyer

Lobbyist
Newspaper reporter
Photographer
Public relations specialist
Secretary

Engineer
Computer hardware
  specialist
Computer software
  specialist
Corporate budget
  manager
Engineer

Patent lawyer
Product manager
Scientist
Technical equipment
  supplier
Technical writer
Technician

Entrepreneur

Advertising specialist
Banker
Entrepreneur
Financier
Lawyer

Manufacturing specialist
Salesperson
Secretary
Security guard
Wholesaler

Lawyer

Accountant
Court clerk
Court reporter
Investigator
Lawyer

Judge
Law librarian
Law office administrator
Legal software specialist
Paralegal

Newscaster

Advertising sales
representative
Athlete
Camera operator
Producer
Makeup artist

Newscaster
Police chief
Political leader
Public relations specialist
Speech coach

Physician

Hospital administrator
Malpractice lawyer
Medical technician
Nurse
Paramedic

Pharmaceutical
salesperson
Pharmacist
Physician
Physician's assistant
Tax adviser

Professor

Editor
Government researcher
Librarian
Philanthropist
Proctor
Professor

Publisher—technical
material
Secretary
Specialist in related
industry
Teaching assistant

CHANGE YOUR JOB—NOT YOUR CAREER

You don't need to give up a satisfying career and turn your life upside down to meet the man of your choice. But if you aren't meeting men in your current job, consider switching jobs within your company, changing to a new sub-specialty, or finding a new job within your industry. A small job change can often increase your chances of meeting that special someone.

Here are ten examples of job changes within the same industry that can enhance your possibilities for meeting men:

1. If you're currently doing market projections, switch to sales. You'll get out from behind your desk and start meeting people.

2. If you're an advertising executive, switch from feminine hygiene products to after-shave lotions.

3. If you're a medical technician, specialize in tests that are administered at the patient's bedside rather than in the laboratory.

4. If you're a corporate accountant, you might not meet men outside the accounting department. Transfer to internal audit, where you'll have the opportunity to examine the other departments in the company.

5. If you write for the lifestyle section of a medium-size newspaper, try switching to the sports section and meet more men.

6. If you sell shoes in a department store, you'll meet more men by selling men's shoes.

7. If you're an engineer, consider technical sales instead of quality control. Get out of the factory and into the public.

8. If you write for a magazine, switch to a business magazine, a sports magazine, a men's magazine, or a magazine for a specific industry that interests you and has a large number of eligible men.

9. If you're a new physician, choose a specialty other than pediatrics or obstetrics and gynecology.

10. If your specialty is hair care, consider using your skills to care for men's hair.

SPECIALIZED JOB SITUATIONS

A short-term job can become a springboard for a long-term love. A part-time job or temporary work may be ideal.

Part-Time Opportunities

If you're looking for love at work, and your job doesn't provide you with sufficient opportunities, consider taking an additional part-time job that is suited to your social needs. This alternative may be preferable to changing your job. Even if your only job is a part-time job, it can give you the opportunities you need to meet men.

Some employers attempt to prevent their employees from taking part-time jobs elsewhere. Accounting firms and police departments are among the worst offenders. However, these restrictions on privacy may be invalid, so it may be worthwhile to challenge or ignore them.

If you're looking for a part-time job, consider teaching an evening course in your chosen career or favorite outside activity. Here are some examples of part-time jobs that can help you meet men:

1. Teach Spanish to businessmen who will be traveling to Latin America.

2. If you are a lawyer, offer a course in malpractice law to physicians.

3. If you are a caterer, offer a course in party-giving.

If your full-time job doesn't have the usual working hours, become a part-time salesperson. A nurse who works from 7 a.m. to 3 p.m. could sell medical equipment and supplies from 3 p.m. until 5 p.m.

You can use a part-time job as a way of finding love as well as earning a living, especially if you're in one of these eight groups: women with children at home, women with children in school, retirees, stay-at-homes and shut-ins, handicapped, students, people living in an area where jobs are scarce, or people working another job full-time.

Here are a dozen of the best part-time opportunities for meeting men:

Sell tools in a garage sale   Almost all of your customers will be able-bodied older men. Offer them coffee and donuts as well as a place to sit and chat.

Cook meals   Many men will enjoy real home cooking in your home. Some of your local businesses—not including restaurants—will let you post your home-cooking sign. The old adage that a way to a man's heart is through his stomach has some merit, so use this opportunity to your advantage.

Teach your ethnic language   He may be a businessman who's traveling to your ancestral home or trying to make sales in your neighborhood. Or he may come from the same background and want to revive his heritage. Either way, you'll be able to get him started talking about himself.

Alter and repair men's clothing   You can use a fitting session as an opportunity to compliment him on his appearance and show him how he can look even better. He associates this type of attention with someone who cares for him.

Provide a shopping service   Buy gifts and groceries for him. You'll be able to use this opportunity to become part of his lifestyle.

Care for others' pets in your home   If he likes the way you care for his pet, he conjures up images of your taking care of him in a loving manner.

House sitting   When he's away, take care of his home. Be sure to reinforce, not disturb, his personal patterns but add some tender loving care and he'll feel you belong there.

Give advice   You can give him advice on restaurants, movies, places to visit, and where to go. You can even put up an "advice" sign on a bulletin board. If you can keep quiet long enough to let him revive and relive his emotions, he'll transfer the positive ones to you.

Run a telephone answering service or wake-up service   Waking up a man by phone isn't the same as being there, but it gives you the chance to plant that idea in his mind.

Coupon exchange   If you cut coupons out of your newspaper, consider running a coupon swap center in your home. When others bring you their coupons, make sure the ones you receive have a higher face value than the ones you give in exchange, and watch out for the expiration dates. You'll start networking as well as cutting your grocery bill. You'll meet men as well as women if you live in a neighborhood where money is scarce.

Give manicures and pedicures   Many men don't cut their own nails, especially their toenails, particularly when they get older. Whether you cut their nails in your home or theirs, you'll be making a good start toward physical closeness.

Telephone solicitor If you sell by phone, you'll have the opportunity to find out about men and spark interest in yourself. You're a step ahead of your competition because you know his real address and phone number and can follow up with another conversation if he interests you.

If you're creating your own part-time job, watch out for government interference. You could be stymied by zoning laws, building codes, and tax rules, so proceed cautiously.

Temporary Work

If you're looking to meet men—and marriage rather than career is your top priority—temporary assignments are the best. If you're a vacation fill-in, you'll see if anyone interests you in just a few weeks. You can leave the company if there's hostility toward your office romance. But if no men interest you, move on sooner. Either way, you can readily switch to another company without ruining your résumé.

Temporary work is appealing to many women (and men). Perhaps you're a mother who does her chores in two days and has three days available for work—and meeting men. Perhaps you're elderly and have energy to work only a few days each week. Or you may need kidney dialysis but are available to work at other times. Yet temporary work is not for everyone. You may be seeking greater career advancement or pension benefits than temporary work allows.

You no longer have to be a clerical worker if you want a temporary job. Even doctors, accountants, computer specialists, engineers, architects, and others can work on a temporary basis. Improve your odds by using your skills in an industry that's primarily male. Become a systems analyst for a contractor or stockbroker, an accountant for a heavy equipment manufacturer or dental clinic, or a physician for a high-tech laboratory or sports team.

Mothers with Children

Women who care for children are working too. House-wives with children work hard, but single mothers with children work especially hard. If you're a single parent devoting your time to caring for your children, how can you find love at work? Many part-time jobs, such as giving pedicures or exchanging coupons, require an hour per day or less. Others, such as clothing repair, can be done while the children are napping. Your children don't have to stand in the way of finding love at work.

The Unemployed

You can't find love at work if you can't find a job, but you might meet your ideal mate in the unemployment line. You can also meet men when you are job hunting, whether they're the interviewers or other job applicants.

HOW MEN ARE USING THEIR JOBS TO MEET YOU

Men aren't sitting idly by while you're going out to meet them. They're trying to meet you, and are sometimes selecting their jobs with female companionship in mind. You may be the pursued as well as the pursuer.

A man who becomes a gynecologist or obstetrician meets many women. A male attorney meets female attorneys much more easily than other men do. However, a man doesn't have to go to law school or medical school just to meet you. Other occupations provide him with easy access to terrific women.

A hairdresser can get to know you more closely than other men can. You probably spend an hour or two with your beautician and chat with him privately. Many women reveal themselves to their hairdressers and fall in love in the process. Your hairdresser sees you "as is," which should make you less aloof. Remember the old slogan, "Only her hairdresser knows for sure." He will have personal contact with you other men can only envy.

A man can sell to businesses that have a large number of women in high places to gain access to these women. He might sell beauty supplies to salons to meet the female owners and managers. He might become a sales representative for a women's clothing manufacturer to meet women buyers. A printing salesmen can meet many terrific women in the publishing and advertising industries. Think about the men you are meeting now and the ways they are using their jobs to meet you.

When you go into a store, you may find men who are working there because they want to meet you. Do you buy your shoes from a man? Many men sell women's shoes so they can meet women with great legs. Is your art dealer interested in you? Working in an art supply shop gives him access to the artsy woman, but any specialty shop attracts a "special" buyer.

Some men enter "female" occupations to meet women. He may become a secretary and try to marry his female boss. Men use this technique to meet women who are lawyers and executives.

Caterers can meet a busy professional woman who has her parties catered. The caterer works closely with her and he is often at the affair itself, overseeing his staff and speaking with the guests. Furthermore, the caterer often sees how the woman lives, what her home is like, what's important to her, whom she wants to impress, and other information men don't easily find out.

A man may become a limo driver to meet terrific women. When you're the only passenger, you may reveal your innermost thoughts to him. A man who becomes a tour guide has ample opportunities to meet women. By the end of the trip, he has time to see which women are interested. The tour guide and limo driver have another advantage. The women may be just visiting the area and not know anyone in town. When the woman is a tourist, she's free from the social conventions of her hometown and more willing to date a man she would rule out at home.

Some men become televangelists to meet large numbers of gullible women. It's like being a gigolo—only worse—for they get money and sex on a larger scale. While you're praying for him, he's preying on you.

Men used to become dance instructors to meet women. Now they're finding better opportunities in the health and sports fields as body builders, ski instructors, sports coaches (golf or tennis), and exercise coaches.

Men take other occupations that enable them to meet the type of women they are seeking. A man who becomes an auditor or bank examiner can meet female bank executives. The office machine repairman has great opportunities to meet female machine operators. A man who sets up a service company can meet many eligible women, especially if he organizes a private nursing service or tutoring service, since most nurses and teachers are women.

CHOOSING THE COMPANY

You may have already selected your career and chosen the type of job you want, but you may be deciding which company is right for you. If you're looking for love at work, here are ten guidelines to follow:

1. Choose a business that is doing well. If it isn't, too much emphasis will be placed on financial survival and there won't be time for love.

2. Discover whether the people are well compensated for the work they do. If they aren't, they're likely to be angry, and that's not the emotion you're looking for.

3. Look for telltale signs of discontent. Unhappy colleagues may bring this unhappiness with them into a relationship, so look for happy employees. Happy people try to spread happiness.

   4. See if the people are working too hard. If they are, they won't have time or energy for love, and chances are you won't either.

   5. Look for career advancement opportunities. As you move upward through the ranks, you'll meet more men.

   6. Look for attitudes that are similar to yours.

   7. Look for a boss who is content with his relationship; then he won't begrudge you yours.

   8. Know their rules concerning socializing with other employees.

   9. Avoid sexist companies where men hate women.

   10. Avoid "lace curtain" companies where women hate men.

CHAPTER 4
Sixty Great Jobs for Meeting Men

If you're looking to meet men on your job or through your job, balance your other career aspirations with this goal, and choose an occupation that helps you reach all of your objectives. Unless you're just starting on your career path, you'll probably be selecting your job from no more than a handful of the ones mentioned here. By examining these jobs and the advantages they provide in meeting men, you'll be able to evaluate any job you're considering.

THE TEN BEST JOBS

Here are ten terrific jobs for meeting men. We've deliberately chosen jobs from all walks of life, so one of these may be right for you:

Bank loan officer
Biographer
Computer salesperson
Hairstylist for men
Instructor in continuing education program
Medical equipment salesperson

Personnel executive for executive search firm
Shoeshiner at a truckstop
Survey taker for a market research firm
Waitress in a breakfast restaurant

Most of these careers require a basic education and specific training, but if these are lacking in your situation, consider becoming a waitress in a breakfast restaurant or a shoeshiner at a truckstop. If your education is not as limited, become a survey taker for a public relations firm or a hairstylist for men.

We'll soon be looking at these ten best jobs as well as fifty more great jobs for meeting men, and five jobs that are surprisingly disappointing.

THE TEN WORST JOBS

Before we look more closely at the ten best jobs, and fifty more great jobs, let's take a look at the worst. The worst conceivable jobs, when it comes to meeting men, are a nun, an office assistant for a lesbian society, a ladies' room attendant, a guard in a women's prison, a beautician in an all-female establishment, or a salesperson in a women's shop. Almost as bad are the opportunities for the day-care worker, sewing-machine operator, telephone operator, and factory assembly worker. If husband-hunting is your priority, move elsewhere.

FIVE SURPRISINGLY BAD JOBS

Here are five jobs that seem like they'd provide great opportunities for meeting men, but don't.

Airline ticket agent
Dentist

Economist
Firefighter
Medical secretary

We'll next be taking a closer look at these five jobs as well as sixty that do provide terrific opportunities for meeting men.

GREAT JOBS
AND NOT SO GREAT

Now examine the sixty jobs for meeting men and the five jobs that are surprisingly poor choices for meeting men. We divided these jobs into ten categories: travel, health care, technology, public safety, financial services, sales and purchasing, real estate, the media, administration and education, and jobs in rural areas.

Travel

Travel agent   If you become a travel agent, you'll meet many men if you select your specialty wisely. Here are some of the best opportunities: In incentive travel, which provides awards for successful sales performance, you'll meet marketing executives. In commercial travel, you'll work with executives and business owners. Either way, you'll be meeting lots of men, but meeting single men is even easier if you're booking them into singles' resorts.

Tour director   You can direct local tours even if you don't live in a tourist area, but the tours will be short and the tourists more than likely will be returning home without you. If you're a tour guide at a tourist location or a tour director on a cruise ship, you'll have more fun and meet more men. In some places, you may be the only friendly and familiar face, so you'll become a "surrogate relative." The group seeks you out, generates warm feelings toward you, and makes you their leader. You'll look particularly desirable to the eligible men. The longer the trip, the better you look!

Pilot Female pilots are still a rarity on commercial airlines, but there's no better access to male pilots. You also can meet male cabin attendants, but be careful in approaching them that you're not charged with sexual harassment. Also, an airline could probably prevent husband and wife or two lovers from working together since domestic disputes could flare up during flights and endanger others.

Your contact with passengers is too brief and lacking in intensity to start a relationship. Irregular hours and hectic travel schedules make it difficult to develop the relationship.

Some men will find you intimidating because they believe that other men are standing in line to date you. If you take the initiative with men, you could be remarkably successful.

Airline ticket agent The airline industry looks so glamorous you might think it's filled with opportunities for meeting your ideal mate, but appearances are deceptive. Ticket agents have little opportunity to meet men because their contact with the public is brief and impersonal. Telephone reservation clerks have even less access to outsiders.

Even at the airport, it's not as easy to chat and flirt with passengers as it used to be. A gate agent checks passengers in, gives seat assignments, and assists passengers in boarding, but too quickly to start a relationship.

To make matters worse, dating a co-worker may be restricted. An airline once prevented husband and wife reservation clerks from working together, and the court sided with the airline.

Airline club hostess In the airline industry, the best job opportunity for meeting men is to work in an airline club. If a man departs frequently from the same airport, he's likely to join an airline club. As a regular member, he'll become friendly with the club staff. The atmosphere is relaxed, comfortable, and conducive to talking and socializing. You can take the initiative and ask questions about his travel, how far and wide his business takes him, and how his family adjusts to his being away. See how easy it is to find out if he's married.

Flight attendant   The days of "coffee, tea, or me" are long gone. Flight attendants rarely have the chance to offer a second cup of tea, let alone anything more personal. Your encounters with passengers are neither long nor intense. Even if you're memorable to a passenger, he won't be memorable to you. He'll be especially reluctant to approach you because he feels he's just another passenger and worries that you will reject him in front of the others. Even if he does initiate contact, he may not know how to follow up with a woman who's on the go.

If you make the effort, you can socialize briefly with passengers and suggest that you get together socially. You can easily break the ice with a simple statement such as "If you enjoy Chinese food, there's a wonderful restaurant in Toledo [Ohio or Spain] you shouldn't miss." The passenger can make the next overture and ask you to join him there or elsewhere.

Also, flight attendants meet as many male pilots as female pilots do.

Restaurant worker   Whether you're a patron or an employee, breakfast is the best time of day to meet men in a restaurant; lunch is second best. Men are often alone or with male colleagues early in the day, but are likely to have female companions later.

Plain Jane down at the donut shop doesn't have any trouble meeting men. For the price of a cup of coffee, a man can become a customer and meet her. Chefs earn more than waitresses, but lose the opportunity to meet customers. That's the trade-off—love versus money.

If you're looking to meet a co-worker, almost any large restaurant will do, but if you're looking to meet customers rather than co-workers, avoid fast-food restaurants that don't have a counter or tables.

Some professions have their own unofficial hangouts. Lawyers often choose a restaurant near the courthouse, while doctors frequent hospital cafeterias. If you're looking for a man with a specific occupation, choose your restaurant accordingly.

Caterer Many businessmen and professionals are too busy to plan their own parties. Some are even too busy to plan their own meals. By helping him with his entertaining needs, you can become part of his life. It's still partially true that the way to a man's heart is through his stomach. You'll come across as a good cook, a skillful organizer, and a caring person, as well as someone with social savvy.

Hotel worker Hotel work can be a source of useful social contacts because most people in the industry change jobs frequently. You work with men in the hotel business long enough to get to know them, but not so long that your co-workers become boring.

If you're looking to meet hotel guests, the best job opportunity is the concierge. The guest may treat you and other members of the staff as his "temporary family." He'll ask you where to go, what to see, even ask you to suggest a doctor if he needs one. Because you're so helpful, the guest may become fond of you. At a later time, you can convert this relationship to a social or romantic one.

Many hotels restrict social contact between staff and guests. If you're interested in dating a guest, you may need to meet him away from the hotel.

One motel chain hires couples only—a rare pro-nepotism rule. After you meet and marry, perhaps the two of you can set up your own hotel!

Shoeshiner If you shine men's shoes, you'll be seeing many feet but meeting few men unless you have a regular clientele. If you shine shoes at a truckstop, you'll see the same drivers each time they come to the truckstop. They'll be looking for a friendly face. If your education is limited, this is one of your best opportunities for meeting men.

Health Care

Dentist   If meeting men is one of your primary goals, don't become a dentist. You'll have access to your patients, but if you're a good dentist with low patient turnover, you'll meet no more than a few hundred new patients every year. It's easier—within ethical rules—for a dentist to date her patients than it is for physicians. Let them be impressed with your "Dr." title. However, negative emotions are undeservedly associated with dentistry and patients are likely to avoid you socially.

You meet other dentists at conventions, but they live in other cities. Even in group practice you meet only a few colleagues.

Eye-care specialist   If you're an eye-care specialist and avoid solo practice, you can meet other eye specialists. But even in group practice, you meet only a few colleagues. If the man of your choice is also an eye-care specialist, your chances are better as an optometrist than as an optician, and even better as an ophthalmologist.

You have good opportunities to meet patients, and can meet thousands per year, especially if your facility is located at a busy shopping mall.

Doctor   Years ago, physicians often married nurses. Today, a male physician often prefers to marry a female physician. If you become a doctor, you will have a higher status than other women he dates and more in common with him. He'll appreciate a mate who shares the pressures and demands on a physician's life. A female doctor has a better chance than a nurse of marrying a male doctor. While more nurses than female doctors marry male doctors, proportionately, female doctors do much better.

For years, women were encouraged to marry a doctor

because he was intelligent and potentially rich. Now, men can appreciate that a woman doctor is a "good catch" for the same reasons.

If you're a physician who's just going into practice, consider having your office in a shopping mall medical clinic. Make it easy for a man to meet you without his claiming to have a heart attack. Another choice is to become the in-house physician for a company in which most of the employees are men.

Medical secretary As a medical secretary, you have access to medical personnel, but they might not accept you as a colleague because secretarial schooling pales in comparison with their studies. If you're looking to marry a physician, don't become a medical secretary. Female doctors and nurses have a strong competitive edge.

You'll meet patients, but your contacts will usually be brief. You'll be able to find out a great deal about the men you meet, but you won't be memorable to them.

Pharmacist Pharmacists have a number of opportunities to meet and marry other pharmacists. Forget solo practice and work for a hospital, pharmaceutical manufacturer, or large drug chain if you're looking to marry a colleague.

A retail pharmacy gives you good access to the public, but they'll have to come to you and may not be in the best of health when they do. You can talk to anyone who walks into your store, hundreds of people each day, yet you're an authority figure as well as a caring specialist. You have the best of two worlds—the sociability of a salesperson and the respect accorded to a medical professional.

Health-care administrator Hospital administrators have easy access to physicians. If the man of your choice may be a doctor, consider a position of power, such as hospital administrator, where the physician cannot take you for granted. If you're looking to meet a colleague, consider working for a health insurance company rather than a hospital.

You'll also be meeting hordes of patients who are angry about the bill or the quality of medical care. If you can resolve their problems, you've got a headstart in building relationships with these patients.

Nurse Nursing is a much better than average occupation when it comes to meeting men. However, some types of nursing are decidedly more favorable than others from a dating standpoint. For nurses, datability is almost the reverse of professional attainment. An examination of the nursing categories demonstrates this curious fact.

Nurses who work in intensive care or critical care have greater responsibility, more training, and higher prestige than ordinary nurses. However, they've fewer opportunities to meet available men on the job. Their patients are seriously ill, and the patients' sons and grandsons are usually distraught and not thinking of dating. Moreover, this specialty is strenuous and stressful, leaving the nurse with limited energy for her social life.

A private-duty nurse in a hospital does better from a dating standpoint than her colleagues who are staff nurses. Her responsibilities are usually modest in comparison, and are often less strenuous and stressful. She meets few eligible men while she is working, but these men are more likely to be potential dates. A man who has a private-duty nurse is more likely to be financially successful, and this might matter to you. Even more important, he's more likely to be thinking of dating. He'll have uninterrupted proximity and the opportunity to talk his way into love with her.

Medical equipment salesperson If you sell medical equipment, you'll have access to the medical community, to other salespeople, and to the scientific and engineering personnel who are responsible for the equipment. Few jobs provide as many opportunities for meeting men.

Technology

Scientist, engineer, or technician In most technical fields, there are far more men than women, but the ratio is not so extreme that men feel you're intruding in an all-male club. Scientists, engineers, and technicians meet many colleagues, especially if they work for a large organization and participate in professional and technical organizations. On the other hand, most careers in science and engineering provide little access to the public.

If you enjoy technology, you have a wide choice of opportunities. You can work in a highly visible area such as television or in isolation with a handful of other technical people.

Technical people tend to be quiet and shy, and usually prefer working with things rather than people. Male engineers will seek you out because they'll find it easier to talk to someone who can relate to them and share their jargon.

If you'd like working in remote locations where there are few other women, consider becoming a petroleum engineer or geologist and working for a petroleum company or mining group. If you're city-oriented, you might enjoy urban surveying, which brings you into contact with real estate developers, contractors, appraisers, and even a few home owners. You'll be able to meet them through the job, but you'll meet few members of the general public.

If you're interested in engineering, but more interested in male engineers, consider becoming a technician. You'll meet them through team assignments, and you'll meet male technicians too.

Technical writer If you enjoy both technology and writing, you can become a technical writer and translate engineering jargon into consumer phraseology. Technical writers have better access to the public than do most other technical specialists and can also meet innovative engineers.

Computer specialist Consider becoming a systems analyst, programmer, or computer service technician. You'll meet other computer people and executives in the industry where you work. You'll be working closely with businessmen as you develop computer programs for them, giving you the opportunity to develop social relationships as you learn about their businesses.

High-tech salesperson   If you sell computers or electronic equipment, you have all the social advantages of working in technology coupled with the social advantages of being in sales. You can meet men who work in computers and electronics, other salespeople, and customers in many different industries.

You don't need a sales personality to sell high-tech products. If you deal in computer products and electronics, you'll have first access to products that intrigue many men. You could say "Phil, they've just come out with a new burglar alarm for cars, and I'd like you to see it." Use your office or home to display electronic goods that amuse men.

Public Safety

Investigator   Private investigators and police detectives meet colleagues and outsiders in various walks of life during the scope of their investigations. What a great way to find out more about the people you meet!

Police officer   The best way to meet policemen is to become a policewoman. You'll also have tremendous access to the general population and can meet almost any man you see, but don't be surprised if he's reluctant to meet you or feels awkward talking to you. After he realizes he's not under arrest, he'll be more relaxed.

Being a police officer has many real disadvantages for meeting men—including stress and odd hours, but there are positives too, beginning with your power to meet the person you choose.

You can meet police officers without becoming one by working as a records clerk in the police station or as a police dispatcher. You'll meet many policemen, but these jobs don't give you a chance to meet the public.

Firefighter If you're looking for love at work, don't look here. Virtually all firefighters are male and have an aversion toward their female co-workers. Sexism creates a negative atmosphere that makes it very difficult for a female firefighter to date the men with whom she works. Peer pressures are even tougher on male firefighters who would want to date their female co-workers. If you become a firefighter, your opportunities to date your co-workers are limited because your fire company is small and there are few opportunities to meet firefighters from outside your group.

Your access to the public is limited except for occasional contact with booster organizations. Of course, you might rescue someone who will respond to this experience with feelings of extreme gratitude and even love, but outside the world of romantic fiction, this hardly seems the way to find your ideal mate.

Inspector You don't have to be an inspector general to generally inspect. Join the health department and inspect restaurants. You certainly will be meeting a large number of owners and managers, all of whom will be trying to impress you.

If you're looking to meet factory managers and industrial engineers, become a safety inspector and inspect facilities for violations. You might wind up checking a few slaughterhouses, but no job is perfect!

Or become a zoning inspector, fire marshall, or property tax appraiser. What a great way to find out how he lives! People you meet will be on the defensive, and that's a drawback, but it doesn't offset the advantage of easy access to large numbers of men.

Financial Services

Financial planner Financial planners are usually selling real estate tax shelters, stocks and bonds, or insurance to their "clients." You don't need an MBA degree, a CPA certificate, or a law degree to hold yourself out as a financial planner. In fact, you don't need any of these qualifications or even a college degree. Nevertheless, many financial planners earn as much as their clients. If you're a financial planner, consider working for a large company with many financial customers. You'll have many opportunities to meet men who value financial success.

You can find out a great deal about a man just from reading his financial data forms and personal data sheets. Then let him reveal his goals and dreams when you meet with him.

Banker If you work for a large bank, you'll meet many other bankers, community leaders, and business executives since banks are often involved in and sponsor social events that promote a good business climate. You may even learn international finance, real estate lending, or money laundering. You'll meet philanthropists, investors, and even drug dealers.

Some banks object to relationships between officers and customers, especially between loan officers and customers. If you're a loan officer, you'll have access to the customer's financial statements and a great deal of personal data. Management may think you're taking unfair advantage if you act socially on that information, so you may need to be secretive about your relationship.

If you're helping a man save or borrow, he'll respect your ability and be grateful for your consideration. This puts you a long way down the road toward a successful relationship.

Accountant Accountants easily meet other accountants, especially in large firms. You'll also meet clients, but dating someone who works for a company your firm is auditing may be viewed as a conflict of interest. If you enjoy accounting but want to meet men, become an internal auditor for your company, or join an accounting firm.

Economist Economists spend most of their time analyzing data, not interacting with people. You might meet other economists, but not the public.

Sales and Purchasing

Insurance salesperson If you're selling insurance, you're not going to meet many other insurance salespeople, but you will meet the public. Say hello to anyone. You can claim you're doing so for business purposes or social purposes, depending on the occasion, but don't forget your business cards. If you can't overcome your shyness, consider becoming an insurance underwriter instead. Let salesmen break the ice for you.

Purchasing specialist If you can greet a sales pitch with a healthy degree of skepticism, consider becoming a purchasing specialist. Technical purchasing is an advantageous sub-specialty if you have an engineering background. If you're in purchasing and he's in sales, there's a conflict of interest whether you're dating or are friends or relatives. Nevertheless, you'll have great opportunities to meet men through your job.

Buyer Buyers often meet wholesalers and distributors at tradeshows. Dating your vendors may be a conflict of interest, but there are many others to meet. You travel a great deal and get to know almost everyone in your product area, from manufacturer to the retail salesperson. With a thimbleful of courage, you can introduce yourself to anyone who interests you and ask about their products or services.

Advertising executive An account executive, media buyer, copywriter, or commercial artist for an advertising agency meets and works with other interesting and talented people. As an alternative, join the sales department of a TV or radio station or magazine or newspaper and sell ads to media buyers at an advertising agency. Advertising's excitement can spill over into starting or enhancing a personal relationship.

Market researcher   Market researchers take surveys and do interviews so they can gain useful information. This process requires teamwork, making it easy to meet your co-workers. If you're on the fieldwork side of market research, you'll have terrific access to the public and you can ask questions that would be considered nosy under other circumstances. It's a fast track to having a man reveal himself.

Car salesperson   A woman who sells cars has a great opportunity to meet men. If you want to meet flashy men, sell sports cars. If you want to meet adventurers, sell off-road vehicles. If you're looking to improve your male–female ratio still further, sell trucks or agricultural equipment.

Manufacturers' representative   You can become a manufacturers' sales representative and get their products into retail stores. If the products are used primarily by men, the buyers are more likely to be male. Consider representing manufacturers of electronic products, building components, or computer accessories.

Retail salesperson   If you work in a department store or other store where you can select your department, you'll have the opportunity to meet men who have the same interests as yours. If you work in the sporting equipment department, you'll meet men who enjoy sports. If you work in housewares, you'll meet gourmet chefs.

Hairstylist for men   If you become a hairstylist for men, you'll meet men one at a time, each with close physical proximity. Treat him much as a wife would by suggesting an attractive hairstyle, showing him how to care for his hair, or telling him what style looks best on him. Fussing over him to look his best gives you an emotional headstart over other women.

Men's clothing salesperson If you're expecting that special man to walk through your door, your expectations may be met if you're working in a men's clothing store. A man who shops for himself can benefit from your ideas about style, what looks best on him, and the proper attire for a particular occasion.

Real Estate

Real estate salesperson Commercial real estate, including office leasing, gives you access to many men. If you choose residential real estate, you'll increase your access to single men by renting apartments rather than selling houses. Let him talk about himself and reveal his present housing needs and future housing goals. He may even tell you how many children he wants. You'll spend hours with a customer, perhaps including lunch together. You'll learn about him quickly. Even if the personal relationship does not "take" on first meeting, you can call him six months or a year later to ask how he's enjoying his apartment or office space or to tell him about a new opportunity. He may call you when he's ready to move. If you're in real estate, you also can meet real estate developers and other real estate professionals.

Architect Architects can meet other architects, especially if they work for large firms. You also work closely with contractors, engineers, bankers, and zoning inspectors. If you do residential architecture, specialize in creative living house plans or bachelor pads. You could be designing your future home.

Interior designer If you're an interior designer, and you concentrate on the commercial side of the business, you'll be meeting large numbers of men. You'll help companies design their office layouts and you'll help executives select their office furnishings. If a particular man interests you, ask him to visit the suppliers with you to select *his* chair.

Apartment manager If you're renting apartments, dealing with tenant problems, and collecting the rent, you'll meet a number of single men. Even if a man doesn't like the apartment you show him, he may like you. If he moves in, proximity and your occasional home-cooked meal can help the relationship build.

The Media

Photographer Photographers have many opportunities to meet the public. These are seven of the best:

- Fashion photographers meet models, including male models.

- Portrait photographers meet important and successful men.

- News photographers meet heroes, politicians, and other newsmakers.

- Medical and scientific photographers meet technical specialists.

- Newspaper photographers meet journalists and celebrities.

- Wedding photographers meet the bride and groom's friends and relatives.

- Sports photographers meet athletes.

Biographer If you enjoy interviewing and writing, you're well prepared to be a biographer, even if this is just a part-time avocation for you. Every man feels that he is unique and has his own story to tell. All you have to do is listen as he reveals his inner thoughts. The more successful the man, the greater his desire to immortalize his words and thoughts through his biography and the more likely he'll have the means to accomplish this goal.

Journalist Many TV and radio journalists date and marry their co-workers, but newspapers often prohibit relationships between their employees. A journalist has access to virtually every member of the public. You could ask people how they feel about an issue or ask them what they'd like to see in your publication or program. If you're writing a magazine or newspaper article about a man, or using a man as a source, you've a good reason to get together with him.

Public relations specialist Introduce your clients, including writers, politicians, and high-profile businessmen, to the media while you're introducing yourself. You'll meet a wide variety of people when you're setting up press events and conferences.

Television producer As a producer, you can meet investors, actors, writers, agents, directors, technicians, other producers, and of course the audience. It's a fast-paced career, but you'll have many opportunities to meet exciting people.

If you're an associate producer, you might pre-interview guests for a TV show, many of whom are eligible men who'll remember you clearly.

Entertainer Make it easy for a man to ask for your autograph and phone number. Go on stage and sing and dance. You will be highly approachable unless your career really takes off. Then your entourage, including your publicity people, will isolate you from the world. But you can always break through that barrier when you want to.

Administration and Education

Association manager You'll meet many men if you

work for a trade association or professional society. Virtually every trade or business has such a group. You can meet members at conventions, seminars, or continuing education courses. If you want a man with a particular occupation, or a man who works for a specific industry, select the organization accordingly. You could become a lobbyist, meeting director, membership director, or editor. You can meet political leaders, meeting planners, and leaders of other organizations as well as members of yours.

Volunteer jobs   A part-time volunteer job can help you meet men, but you may wind up with menial tasks. You can get involved with a museum, historical society, architectural preservation group, or community action group, and change jobs without getting bad marks on your personnel record.

Secretary   If you're a secretary, you'll gain insight into how your boss thinks, as well as his habits, talents, and attitudes. You'll become very important to him, almost "family," since he depends on you and will confide in you.

Politician   Run for political office or assist a candidate in a campaign. It's a great way to meet people, especially those with leadership qualities. If your candidate wins, you may have a whirlwind social life for the years your candidate is in office.

Lawyer   As an attorney, you'll meet clients and other lawyers. By choosing a specialty, you can select the type of men you'll meet. Unless you're looking for a felon, criminal law is not your best bet for spouse-hunting. If you practice tax law, you'll meet accountants and bankers as well as high-income individuals. Contrary to what you might think, divorce work is not the best way to meet a potential spouse. Your client may have "another woman" who is the reason for his divorce, or feel so guilty that his marriage failed that it'll take several years for him to recover. That's too long to wait.

You can work with lawyers without becoming one.

Consider becoming a law office administrator or legal assistant. You'll rarely meet the public, but you'll meet plenty of lawyers.

School administrator   If you're an administrator, you can meet principals, deans, and other administrators as well as teachers and critics of the school system. You have high visibility, power, and prestige, all of which make it easier for you to meet men.

Educator   If you teach in primary or secondary school, teaching is one of the worst professions for meeting men. However, adult education is a whole different story. You'll teach adults who are willing learners, you'll receive recognition and respect from your classes, and you'll look desirable to many of the men. They'll consider you bright if you can teach them.

Why not teach in college part-time? You don't need a Ph.D. to marry the man of your choice. You'll meet colleagues and interesting students as a college teacher.

Librarian   Librarians used to have their noses in books, shushing patrons who dared talk in their sanctum. Today, many libraries have become media centers and the image of librarians has changed accordingly.

The rapid increase in information has led to the growth of private libraries for business, government agencies, and major organizations. If you're a librarian, you can select the men you want by the library you choose.

Meeting planner   Forget mammoth conventions. Instead, plan many small meetings in which you can meet and talk to the participants. Meeting planners specialize in tradeshows, conferences, and shareholder meetings. There's a constant flow of movers and shakers of your community, and you'll keep in contact with caterers, sound technicians, the press, hotel staff, and those you count on to help you set up a meeting.

Personnel specialist   The personnel files let you know

who is truly eligible. A position in human resources enables you to find out basic information you want to know about many men. You can make your choice from among the best in every division of the company. Then use the information about the man to guide the conversation to topics he'll enjoy.

Executive recruiter Consider becoming an executive recruiter. If you have a certain kind of man in mind, whether an advertising executive, a computer expert, or a hotshot salesman, then specialize in recruiting that kind of talent. This job certainly gives you access to people who otherwise are hard to meet, and the chance to use their résumés to screen them in advance. You'll also be able to meet the people who *hire* the advertising executives, computer experts, or hotshot salesmen.

Busybody Being a busybody is a job, even if you don't get paid for it. If you live in a condo, join the owners' association; if you live in a house, join the homeowners' association. If you live in a rental apartment, join a tenants' group to meet lawyers, landlords, and neighbors. If you're an activist for any cause, you'll meet other folks who are passionate about the same things you are.

Jobs in Rural Areas

Farm equipment repairperson If you have mechanical ability and live in a rural area, one of your best opportunities for meeting men is to repair their farm equipment.

Operator of rural store If you can handle heavy workloads at some times, and extreme quiet at others, consider running a feedstore or a general supply store connected to a grain elevator. Either way, you'll be meeting hardworking farmers.

Farmer Many women who grew up on farms have

moved to the city. Not surprisingly, many farmers are now seeking wives from nonfarming backgrounds.

Veterinarian   If tractors and plows don't appeal to you, don't despair. A veterinarian or veterinary assistant who moves to a rural area has tremendous opportunities.

CHAPTER 5
Expanding Your Horizons

Expand your dating horizons. Your job will bring you in contact with many men in different walks of life. Take advantage of this diversity in selecting your dates. Your ideal mate may be just a glance away, but only if you're looking in many different directions. If marrying up is one of your goals, you now have access to men that will enable you to turn your goal into reality. However, if you have a successful career, you don't need a man for his money. Once you separate the concepts of men and money, it's easy to expand your horizons.

Some women think they are too "good" to marry a blue-collar worker, but this snobbishness may keep them from happiness. When you're open-minded, you'll gain the opportunity to meet many men. If you've excluded blue-collar workers as potential mates, it's well worth giving them a second look.

BLUE-COLLAR WORKERS

Many successful male executives spend their evenings with waitresses, manicurists, or salesclerks rather than with women who are their professional equals. Similarly, you can date blue-collar workers even if you're a successful executive.

Many blue-collar workers are bright, interesting people who learned a trade as a fast path from adolescence into the working world. Not everyone could postpone his financial needs for college and graduate school. Blue-collar workers often have outside interests, and, unlike high-pressure executives, have the time to pursue them instead of bringing work home. Why not marry a man who repairs computers instead of programming them?

To meet a blue-collar worker, you can go into a blue-collar occupation yourself. You might enjoy construction work or equipment repair. You'll also gain access to blue-collar workers if you take a job with a manufacturer.

If you'd like to meet taxi drivers, become a dispatcher. You can meet car mechanics by getting a clunker and taking it around for repairs. You can use your sink as a lure to meet plumbers or your cabinets to meet carpenters.

DATING YOUR SUBORDINATES

If you're an executive, you'll face social pressures at work that make it difficult for you to date a subordinate. If he's at a lower level in the company, your male colleagues may misconstrue your interest in him and assume that you're uncomfortable at your career level. They'll make your climb up the corporate ladder even more difficult. Be prepared to let your colleagues know what you find attractive about your lover. You may have to brag about him in order to dispel these male myths.

It's even riskier to date someone on your staff than it is to date one of your colleagues, so keep the relationship secret at first. Management may doubt your loyalty to the company, and jealous co-workers may accuse you of favoritism toward your assistant. Total discretion is absolutely necessary since you're between two hostile camps.

Are You Overwhelming?

The man of your choice might be below you professionally or at a lower level in the company. Here are some specific strategies for that situation.

A man won't pursue a woman he considers too far above him. If you want a man, make sure he feels you're within reach. You'll need to open the door for him to walk into your life beyond being a business acquaintance.

If your position at work is higher than his is, reveal just enough information about yourself to create interest, but not so much that you'll overwhelm him. Guestimate his credentials and slip in enough of your own to approximate his. Save some aces for later in case you'll need them to respark his interest.

If you don't tell him anything about yourself, he may think that you're a snob or so far above him that you won't chat with him again. If you tell him too much, you could be too impressive and too intimidating. Start with a few facts about yourself and ask him similar facts about his background. Give him the chance to tell you about his accomplishments. Then indicate that you're impressed with what you've heard.

If he meets you at work, you may have automatically established your credentials. If you and he are both in the same profession, it shouldn't be necessary to show your credentials. However, colleagues sometimes test each other as part of their jockeying for position within the organization. Be prepared.

Be Realistic

If you want to find love at work, transcend your childhood fantasies and let the workplace bring reality into your world. You're not Snow White, Cinderella, or Sleeping Beauty

Would you marry a man whose work habits you know, whose paycheck may be less than yours, whose career opportunities may be limited? If you are genuine when you say you are looking for companionship, then your answer to this question should be "yes."

There is a big difference between what people do and what they say they do. Many women subconsciously revert to selection criteria that are no longer appropriate and reject the very men who could give them lifelong companionship. Take a close look at your dating history and consider whether the men you're dating meet your real needs.

Some women are looking for men who are good providers, yet they're supporting themselves more than adequately. Some women are looking for men who have dominant personalities, but they'd never agree to be dominated. Know yourself before you start your quest. You do have needs, and with some perseverance you can find a man who fulfills these needs.

IF YOU'RE THE BOSS'S DAUGHTER

Until recently, a number of men gained a business and a wife by marrying the boss's daughter. This is still happening, especially when a chauvinistic business owner is reluctant to turn the company over to his daughter.

If your dad has a business and you're expecting to leave the business world for a number of years to raise a family, having your husband run the business may initially look ideal. But the reality is often otherwise. What if you want to reenter the business world? What if you have better ideas about how the company should be run?

The key is voting stock. As your husband moves up the executive ladder, make sure you're moving up the ownership ladder. Even if you're not active in the family business at that time, you can still be a member of the board of directors. You don't need to avoid take-charge men since you can retain ultimate control.

MARRYING UP

Years ago, a woman might have taken a lowly clerical occupation in close proximity to rich men in the hope of marrying one. These opportunities are far fewer now.

Social Mobility

Beware of taking a subservient occupation. Don't diminish your education and experience in your job search. Men are not looking to marry down. They once had to, but this is no longer the case. If men do marry down, they prefer a junior member of the same profession, not a nonprofessional assistant. A male executive prefers a female executive, not a clerk-typist. If you want to marry a well-educated, articulate executive, your best bet is to become a well-educated, articulate executive yourself.

Class-consciousness is increasing. The success of the women's movement will eventually lead to greater class distinctions and less social mobility. Daughters of professionals are becoming professionals and marrying professionals. Fewer higher level men will be left over for nonprofessional women.

Traditional Attitudes

Some women are looking to marry "up," to marry a man who will be the principal breadwinner if not the sole support of the family. These women are finding themselves at a competitive disadvantage. They fail to attract men who are above them and have the financial resources to support them. Women with these old-fashioned attitudes reject male colleagues who earn what they earn. They view their male co-workers negatively as prospective mates since these men do not fulfill their "upward bound" fantasies.

You may have learned about marrying up at your mother's knee, so you must consciously reject it if you take your equality seriously. But if marrying up is your priority, we'll show you how.

MARRYING THE BOSS

If you could love a rich man as easily as a poor man, think about marrying the boss. You could wind up being the boss too. Many a male business leader is looking for a woman who will share his life completely, the boardroom and the bedroom.

You can use your job to become indispensable to him. To begin with, you'll need business skills he doesn't have. If you're an MBA, you'll be especially appealing to a man who started his business from scratch, a streetwise shirtsleeve type who lacks your formal training. If you have practical experience, you'll be most appealing to a man who has an MBA.

If the man you're attracted to is your boss, the greatest obstacle you may face is his idea that since he's superior to you at work he's also superior in a personal relationship. Solve that problem by building yourself up, and—where necessary—knocking him down by pointing out past errors he has made.

Opposites do attract, but only initially. If you want to build a relationship, you should have a great deal in common with the man. Since both you and he are likely to be hard at work, that something in common is probably job-related.

If you're looking for a businessman, an executive, or a professional, you've got to be able to relate to him on a mental level, not just appeal to him physically. Let him know that you can be, and are willing to be, his mental companion.

Increasing Your Knowledge

Your boss doesn't have a monopoly on gathering knowledge or thinking power. You too can think and express ideas, even brilliant ones! If you ask your boss an intelligent question about what's happening in his world, beyond what you might know from your job, you'll rise several pegs in his estimation. The more intelligent questions you ask, the higher he'll rate you. When you ask him a question he doesn't know the answer to but should, you'll be testing his mental frontiers and he'll respect your capacity to think. This strategy should help your career advancement too.

For further impact, watch business television programs and read the business section of your newspaper. Be prepared to discuss more with your boss than the price of the company's stock.

Whenever possible, let your boss know that you're impressed with his good ideas. Nodding, smiling, or expressing "That's a great idea" certainly conveys the message. Get him in the habit of looking for your approval. Let him know that you're so self-assured that you dare pass judgment on his ideas. It may irk him a bit, or he may ignore your approvals, but whenever he needs a few words of encouragement because he's had a rough day, he'll seek your views.

Conversely, if his idea seems erroneous to you, withhold approving comments. He may ask why you've said nothing. In that case, tell him that this idea is not as good as his others and give your reasons. You've really made it if he uses you to finalize his thoughts.

Piercing the Physical Barrier

Because a man usually was brought up by a woman who fussed over his wardrobe and grooming, he'll view your attention to his appearance as a sign of concern, loyalty, or even affection. If he'll be meeting with his superiors or powerful clients, suggest that he wear his dark blue suit or trim his hair before the meeting to have a more executive look. Then take the next step and straighten his tie or brush the lint off his jacket to condition him to come to you for approval. Don't view these actions as being subservient. His mother fussed over him and she wasn't subservient. The key is physical proximity that pierces the boss–subordinate relationship.

Acquiring Sophistication

Show some savvy in areas beyond work. Suggest restaurants he may want to use to impress his clients. Keep a nonfiction book that you are currently reading on your desk and be prepared to discuss the ideas in it. If your boss is young or middle-aged, books that deal with money or sex will catch his interest. If he is an older man and rather comfortable, books on culture may pique his interest. If you want to introduce the idea that love can occur at work, keep a copy of this book on your desk.

Of course, you can begin your conversation with general topics that lead to personal conversation. On Friday, mention good movies or timely activities he might enjoy. On Monday, ask him if his weekend was pleasant. The greater the variety of topics you show interest in, the more interesting you'll be to him.

Becoming His Protégée

Can you find happiness—and career success—with a senior executive? You may be able to, if he's your mentor and you're his protégée. A mentor is a sponsor within the corporate framework who helps the protégée learn and move up, yet this is more than just a business connection.

A professor had a wager than he could teach a female street urchin the Queen's English and then pass her off as royalty. He succeeded, but fell in love with her in the process because of the effort, time, and emotions he invested in her. This is the story of *My Fair Lady*. While it's extreme, it does illustrate the advantage of being a protégée.

When you're working with a man who interests you, look for his skills or his knowledge that he'll gladly teach you. If he spends even as few as several hours with you, that's enough for him to feel a sense of camaraderie and caring. You become special to him.

Observe his enthusiasm and ease in dealing with his responsibilities. Discover whether he's at his best dealing with people, thinking up new strategies, carrying out details, or organizing what must get done. Whatever he is good at, there's a chance that he'll enjoy discussing his strengths and giving you useful tips. You'll increase the amount and intensity of his emotions for you by continuing your interest in his work.

A man is often reluctant to be a mentor to a woman because he fears his peers will assume that they're having an affair, especially if he meets with her after business hours. He may also refrain from these get-togethers to avoid becoming attracted to her.

A male executive might find it uncomfortable to have a mentor–protégée relationship with a female staff member, worrying that she'll misunderstand his interest. Ironically, fear of sexual harassment charges dissuades men from helping women advance in their careers.

A romantic relationship between mentor and protégée may possibly be unprofessional and unbusinesslike. However, it also may be a good way to find love at work. Mentor–protégée behavior codes may eventually evolve, like those for doctor–patient, lawyer–client, or teacher–student relationships. In the meantime, make use of the opportunities.

Dating His Boss

You know there are some obstacles to dating your boss, but there are different problems in dating your boss's boss.

Dating someone in the chain of command can cause problems even when one person does not report to the other. But if you date your boss's boss, you'll create an especially awkward position for the person in the middle who is your supervisor and his subordinate. This is true whether this middle-management person is male or female. The person in the middle will feel reluctant to report honestly to his or her boss—your lover—about your work output. If this is your story, give your boss an honest day's work and don't try to pull social rank. Otherwise, all three of you could be seeking new jobs.

Marrying the Owner's Son

Instead of marrying the boss, why not marry the boss's son? Some men come from a business background but have no interest in a business career. He may not want to run Daddy's business because he prefers to be a lawyer, sculptor, or professor. Yet his family wants to keep the business in the family. A number of women have married into business families and taken over both. If you're willing to be president while your father-in-law is chairman, think about marrying the owner's son.

Here are some specific strategies you can use: The son may currently be working in the business, but not by choice. Meet him and help him look good in the business—but not too good. Be his advocate in dealing with his family. Help him interpret the balance sheet or devise the marketing plan. Make sure he is dependent on you and knows it. Encourage him in his nonbusiness endeavors. "You're much too good a sculptor to spend time with sales data."

Because you're dating him, you'll gain access to his father. When you're with his father, talk business. Don't get trapped in the kitchen with his mom unless she's a business-woman too. Tell "Dad" how exciting his business is. Your biggest threat may be his sister who has business ambitions of her own.

Men have married the boss's daughter for years. Why shouldn't a capable woman marry the owner's son and use the same path to business success?

DEVELOPING YOUR PERSONAL STRATEGY

If you have a position of power, or if you're wealthy, you may wonder whether a man is really interested in *you*, or whether he's interested in what you can do for him. Wealthy and powerful men are often skeptical of the women they meet, and women who have acquired wealth or power are just as skeptical.

The wealthy and powerful are afraid of being used, so they eliminate from consideration anyone who could be in a position of using them. Their usual approach is to become snobbish. As a defense mechanism, a wealthy or powerful woman insists on dating up, not down.

The talk-show host won't date a man who is a musician. She fears that he wants to date her so that he can get on her show. Instead, she wants to date the station manager or a newspaper publisher.

The judge won't date a male lawyer who might appear before her. She fears that he's interested in her so that he can get a more favorable judgment. Instead, she wants to date the appellate court judge or the mayor.

The woman business owner usually won't date one of her suppliers. She fears that he's really interested in making a sale. To spare herself that indignity, she'd rather date her banker or the owner of a larger business.

All three miss out on a lot of fine people who are at their level or are below them. Even worse, by dating up, they give the impression that they're trying to use their dates. This impression is probably false, but the newspaper publisher is concerned that the talk-show host is trying to get her own column. The higher court judge worries that the lower court judge is dating him so that her rulings won't be reversed. The banker is concerned about the owner of the small business. Since they're also afraid of being used, they may avoid these interesting and exciting women. Since she has already ruled out men below her, she often winds up alone.

There ought to be a better way, and fortunately there is:

First, date him, but let him know you must bend over backward to maintain your objectivity. Tell him that a man who dates you would be ineligible to be on your show or sell products to your company. Then, if he does decide to date you, you might decide to relax the prohibition at a later date.

Second, you can tell the genuineness of his interest if the relationship becomes romantic and then sexual. If he really isn't interested in you, his performance will decline rather rapidly.

Third, interview the man to discover his attitudes. Ask him about his business or his career and how important they are to him. Ask him about the other women in his life and look for patterns in his relationships. Then let him tell you about his priorities.

INCREASING YOUR SELF-CONFIDENCE AT WORK

If you view yourself as attractive, successful, and eligible, each male co-worker is likely to view you in the same light. He has high standards for his future wife. Don't let your job make you appear less sophisticated, educated, or competent than you are. We've spoken with thousands of men over the past two decades, and not one has ever said he wanted to *marry* a dummy or a loser.

Self-confidence

Start by improving your feelings of confidence. When you're wearing an expensive dress, you'll walk prouder and more confidently than when you're in your cleaning outfit, yet you're the same person. There is no reason why you can't always be wearing that expensive outfit in your mind. Develop an air of confidence that is strong enough that you feel it most of the time. If you need a little practice, dress in your finery for a week. After seven days, you've got the habit of feeling good about yourself. With a little self-nurturing, you won't slack off. People will start treating you with more dignity, and you'll further increase your self-esteem

Respect

Be respectful to your superiors in the hierarchy, but not obsequious. Don't fawn or gush over the management. Use their titles only when necessary, but then refer to yourself in a more formal manner using your last name rather than your first.

Let people call you by your first name or nickname only after you know them. They'll feel you're special, not just another worker. Unless you're high in the pecking order, muster as much importance to yourself as possible. If you can give yourself a title, do so. "Maintenance Engineer" sounds a lot more impressive than "handyman" or "handy-woman." Conversely, if you're a power player in the organization, when someone you like refers to you by your formal title and name, invite him to call you by your first name.

If for the time being you can't get as much recognition on the job as you need to enter the social circles you want, these are two strategies that should help: One is to go back to school and present yourself as struggling for the credentials you're seeking, even if the training will take many years. The other is to apply for a better job now and hope that your experience can see you through. Even applying for the better job indicates a positive self-image.

Outside Achievements

You can also better your image at work by interests or achievements outside of work. If you're a champion swimmer, talk about an exciting match, tell a fellow he should consider swimming as he is built for that sport, subscribe to a magazine for swimmers and display it at the office, or display a medal you've won. Let people know things about you that you're proud of.

Professional Personality

Develop a "professional" personality by not revealing your emotional reactions. You'll appear composed and sophisticated by not allowing anyone to push you into expressing great misery or great joy. Don't say "yippee" when you get a promotion or Mr. Right asks you out. Don't let them see you jump for joy, and don't let them see you sweat.

Educated Speech

Speech is a common indication of a person's status, but because speech is primarily a habit, people don't really think about the best word to use. Instead, they use the first word that comes to mind, even if they're people of extraordinary position. The more "ordinary" you are, the more thought you should give to your vocabulary and use the best word you know. By putting your mind in gear before you speak, you could raise your status with speech. Saying "I'm pooped" sounds vulgar compared to "I'm exhausted."

Speak cautiously and present yourself as a woman who knows the importance of having others hear her words. This self-regard influences others to have a higher opinion of you and is also very prudent. At work, it's likely that someone can easily overhear your conversations, so give your opinions cautiously.

Your rate of speech can also type you. If you speak slowly, you could be considered a slow thinker. If you speak too fast, you might be thought of as compulsive or scatterbrained. Keep your rate of speech calm and consistent. To practice, pace yourself with the speech of the news commentators.

Your Reading Material

Become familiar with the jargon of your industry. Read the basic texts and trade publications that cover new trends, who's who, and what's what in your business. Also read the business magazines and professional journals. This may not be easy from a time standpoint because you also have to keep up in your own field. If a man is pursuing you with equal vigor, he'll also be learning about what you're doing. It's a good sign when you both see how your field and his could tie in to each other.

Many women's magazines convey a negative attitude about men that will harm both your working and dating relationships. Their standard approach is to blame all relationship problems on men. Of course, not all women's magazines do this, but some magazines for single women are the worst culprits. Avoid them if you're seeking love at work.

The man knows that women's magazines are often sexist. He'll react as negatively to your reading these magazines as you would if he read ordinary men's magazines and judged you by their criteria.

The most strident women's magazines are the worst. Feminism shouldn't mean man-hating, but there's a small but very vocal segment of women for whom it does. If you're interested in marriage, avoid these publications.

Compliments

Don't build someone else up at your own expense. If you're an advertising copywriter, don't tell a colleague he is the finest ad writer you know. If you say that, you're telling him that he is a better copywriter than you are. Compare him favorably to others, not to yourself. Don't put yourself down when you're building him up.

When you're complimented, don't diminish the compliment. If someone says, "Janice, I'm really impressed with your sales forecast," respond with "I'm delighted you find it useful," not "It was nothing."

CHAPTER 6
Planning for Office Encounters

You can meet men at work if you know where to look and how to make yourself memorable. Here are some specific strategies for using the workplace to your advantage.

WHERE TO MEET AT WORK

If eligible men surround you in your work environment, use work-related activities to meet them. Socialize during coffee breaks or lunch and after work. You can also meet men when you're commuting or enjoying company-sponsored recreation.

Coffee Breaks

Coffee breaks provide a good meeting opportunity, whether your company has a refreshment cart or snack room. Either way, bring plenty of change. Unlike women's wallets, men's wallets don't have a change section, so men don't usually bring change with them. There is no harm in offering to treat a man who is fumbling for his change.

Instead of having the same snack each day, ask your co-workers what looks tasty today. Use the refreshment cart as a prop to begin chatting with the men around you.

At Lunch

Lunchtime can be a great opportunity to meet eligible men. Don't waste your lunch hour going shopping for clothes, shop for a mate instead.

If your company has an executive dining room, and you're eligible to use it, great, but the employee cafeteria also provides good opportunities. A bachelor may be having his only hot meal of the day, so make sure you don't skip lunch.

Many of you miss the chance to meet people because you sit with the same clique each day. If you want a man to join you for lunch, make sure there's an empty seat next to you. If you want a particular man to join you, move your papers aside or just invite him to join you.

As an alternative, join him. How do you know when you're welcome? What if there are no other tables? What clues is he giving off, and how can you pick up on these clues? You may know his reputation for friendliness, so start there. You're far more likely to be welcome if he's sitting alone. If he's with someone, male or female, don't invite yourself to join him.

If your company doesn't have its own lunchroom, don't despair. You still can meet your co-workers at lunch. In fact, your chances may be even greater since your actions will receive less scrutiny. The men may go to nearby restaurants on their lunch hour, so choose these restaurants and run into the men you want. You could even ask for a ride.

Employee's Lounge

Use the employee's lounge to meet men. Obviously, by the "lounge" we mean a real lounge, not a restroom. The employee's lounge leads to relaxed informality. It's easier to start a conversation here if you don't have a business excuse that brings you to his desk.

Some people use a cigarette as a signal that they're relaxing, but there are better signals. Do a crossword puzzle and ask "What's a twelve-letter word that's used in music or debating and is also a bed covering?"

After Work

If you and your co-workers stop in for a drink after work, use this opportunity to meet men. Select a place that serves food and soft drinks as well as liquor. If you're working normal hours, and going to the bar after work, you'll be there during happy hour. Happy hour usually includes a buffet of appetizers or snacks, perhaps meatballs or nachos. But once happy hour ends, the hardcore drinkers remain. You should be leaving too, so treat the end of happy hour as your curfew.

One advantage to the happy-hour bar is that you can lessen some of the barriers even if you're dressed for work. You can literally let your hair down. But even the happy-hour place has its drawbacks. You may be waiting for an alcoholic to hit on you. Stay near the food, not the bar, to minimize this risk. Don't confuse after-work happy-hour hangouts with late-night singles bars. They should be avoided.

Chances are you'll be going to the pub in a group. Try to make this a coed group. An all-female group is intimidating to a man who is by himself, but if you're in a group of women you may have some success with your group joining a group of men.

Office Parties

Office parties can be an effective way of meeting people, but there are two major drawbacks: inebriation and the public nature of the event. However, you still have a chance to say "hello" to those you don't see often and renew their interest in you.

Business Parties

Many of you socialize with your co-workers. You not only see them for lunch or after work, you invite them to parties in your homes. You may also be inviting vendors or customers. Go to—and give—these parties to let people know you're friendly. The next week a fellow can say, "I saw you at a party but didn't get a chance to introduce myself."

Professionals tend to socialize with colleagues in the same profession and sometimes in the same specialty. Tax lawyers often party with other tax lawyers. Physicians golf with other physicians. Computer experts gather with other computer people. Everyone else is just a layman or a civilian as far as they're concerned. If you belong to one of these professions, take advantage of the club-like atmosphere to socialize with your peers.

We certainly recommend business parties. That's how we met.

Elevator

If your building has an elevator, you'll have an additional opportunity to meet men. It may be your only opportunity to meet men who work for other companies in the same building. Say good morning to everyone as you get on.

Don't expect or encourage special treatment because of your gender. If you do, you'll appear aloof and unapproachable. Don't expect men to let you exit first when you're in the back of the elevator. You are not a princess, and they're not your servants.

Instead, show as much courtesy to a man as you would show to another woman. If you're in the elevator, and a man is coming toward it, hold the door open for him. Don't just hold the button, hold the door. Let him see your effort.

You'll get rewarded with a smile, a thank-you, and a friendly feeling toward you. Turn this positive attitude into an introduction.

Using Your Car

It finally happened. Mr. Right came over to your desk to speak with you. He even asked you for a ride home! The only trouble is that your car is a mess with chewing gum wrappers on the floor, lint on the front seat, an unopened box of disposable diapers on the backseat, and children's toys everywhere. Men generally like children, but not an overabundance of children's things in the car. Keep your children's toys and paraphernalia in the trunk, so that you're ready when he asks you or when you take the initiative and offer him a ride.

Most men like cars, and your choice of a car can help you to attract men. Sports cars and antique cars will draw some men to you, but will intimidate other men because of their cost. Don't assume you will always be taking his car. Men are offended by this attitude.

If you're looking for a man whose height is more than a few inches different from your own, get a car with split seats so that you can be comfortable when he drives and he's comfortable when you drive.

Have jumper cables in your car. They'll make your trip safer and give you the chance to offer help to others.

Parking Lot

If your company has a parking lot, you can use it in meeting men, especially if parking spaces aren't reserved.

In some companies, where there are no reserved parking spaces, the first employees to arrive park closest to the building. If the executives arrive later, they'll be parking farther back. If these executives are predominantly male, you can meet them by parking farther away from the building than you otherwise would. You'll be parking near more of these men and meeting more of them when you leave work.

Air Travel

Join an airline club. Spend your money on club membership, not on paying for first-class or business-class tickets. These clubs are private lounges with many travelers. Most are men traveling on business, so don't forget your business cards.

Some airline flights are better than others. Short-distance shuttles such as New York–Boston, New York–Washington, and Los Angeles–San Francisco are usually the best bet.

One way to get a man's attention is to have something interesting with you, like this book. Make it easy for him to start chatting with you.

Athletics

If you're a good athlete, you've got the inside "track" to meeting men at many companies. Squash (the game, not the vegetable) is a real plus in some companies. Elsewhere, you'll do better with tennis, golf, or ping-pong. Invite him to jog with you.

Company Teams

Participate actively on a company team if you're competent in some facet of the sport. When your co-workers are playing golf or tennis, or even touch football, join in. Let them view you as an asset to the team, but don't play if you'll be in the way. Don't force your way onto a team by virtue of your business position. As a general rule, if you can play as well as most of the women and some of the men, participate. If not, cheer for your team. They'll love your spirit.

All-women teams are a different matter. You're not going to meet many men except for a few male groupies. When it comes to husband hunting, the women's bowling league isn't a good use of your time. If you enjoy bowling, join a coed team instead.

Joining the Company

When you first join a company, you have extra opportunities for husband-hunting. You have access to everyone, even those you'll later discover are off-limits. Make the most of your employee orientation and provide your own unofficial employee orientation too. Visit departments you might not have contact with on a daily basis but have reasons to visit now, including payroll, personnel, and employee benefits. Introduce yourself to everyone and follow through with repeat visits to the men who interest you. Later, volunteer to take new employees on their orientation tour.

BEING MEMORABLE AT WORK

It's not enough for you to remember the people you meet, they need to remember you. Here are some things about you that might be memorable: looks, clothing, conversation, name, and job. Of course, being the best at something will make you memorable, but so will being the worst.

Status and power within the organization create great visibility. You may be better off with a low-level management position than with a high-level staff position if you're seeking visibility.

The boss is always memorable. Women are still attracted to male power to a much greater extent than men are attracted to female power, but power makes anyone memorable. First, you'll be physically memorable because you're unique. Second, your conversations will carry greater intensity to the people you meet when you have organizational power.

Selecting Your Wardrobe

Let your clothes be an asset in finding love at work. You may need to dress in a businesslike manner to maximize your success potential, yet you can also dress in a friendly manner that maximizes your appeal to men.

If you're an executive, you probably wear an outfit that reflects your authority and creates a barrier between you and your subordinates. In many industries, this outfit is the power suit. You may need to wear high-quality clothes to demonstrate your level in the corporate hierarchy. However, just because you impress your company's directors doesn't mean you're impressing potential dates. If you select your outfits wisely, you can impress both.

Looking businesslike and authoritative often means wearing layers of clothing, but each layer is another barrier. You can wear that power suit, even with a tie, yet take your jacket and tie off and look attractive to men. Wear a blouse that softly follows your body's form and isn't frilly or ruffled. The material should look pleasant to touch, so you can look friendly and approachable when you want to. Choose success-oriented colors that are also friendly colors, especially blue, red, black, and white. Avoid purple, pink, orange, and most shades of green in the office. Except for accessories, limit yourself to one or two solid colors or a simple pattern. Avoid fashion unless it meets these standards.

Accessories

Your job may limit the extent to which your clothes can make you memorable at work. If you must wear a uniform, you're greatly limited in your use of clothing to be memorable, but you can select memorable accessories.

Your hairstyle can help you look friendly. Long hair is

advantageous, but it should not be longer than the hair of
other women at your job level. Pick a hairstyle that's neat
but isn't letter-perfect. A slightly tousled look makes a man
imagine touching your hair. Encourage that thought. Hair in
a bun has no great appeal, so be prepared to let your hair
down when the occasion arises.

High-quality clothes and accoutrements can be sexy
power symbols. Select a shoe style that sets off your curva-
ceous legs, but lets you walk rapidly and quietly. Low or
medium heels are best for most women.

If you must let others know you're in the big league,
use accoutrements to show your power, including your
expensive watch and your fancy pen. They're your "power
tools." In contrast, minimize jewelry, regardless of your
position in the company. If you're single and searching,
avoid rings altogether. They signal to men that someone
special is already in your life.

Using Nails and Makeup

Nails that are neat and manicured are a plus, but long
fingernails don't belong in the office. Your hands should look
functional, capable of operating a computer, peeling carrots,
playing tennis, and partaking of frolic and fun.

Minimize makeup for both business and social purposes. Heavy makeup is inappropriate at work unless you're
on camera or getting on in years. Keep lipstick and makeup
off his collar when you're at work.

How to Dress

Follow these two basic rules if you want to be both
impressive and friendly at work:

1. Dress friendly, but not too friendly. Don't look
provocative.

2. Dress up. Notice what your female supervisors wear and dress in a similar manner.

Specific Advice

Barriers make a woman look unapproachable, which is the opposite of dressing friendly. If you're secure in your business position and you're looking for love, let some barriers down. Your wardrobe has both business barriers and nonbusiness barriers. You may not be able to get rid of business barriers, but you can get rid of nonbusiness barriers. Here are ten specific ideas for dressing friendly at work:

1. If you're going to wear slacks to work, avoid tight pants. They're appealing to men, but aren't businesslike. Baggy slacks are even worse because they're not even appealing to men.

2. A low-cut dress will generate male attention, but it isn't any more businesslike than tight pants.

3. Don't wear gloves in the office.

4. Don't wear sunglasses in the office.

5. Don't wear a hat in the office.

6. Simple monograms may be both attractive and impressive.

7. Use red or clear nailpolish at work.

8. If you wear a sweater to work, make sure it has a solid color.

9. Don't smoke or chew gum at work. Neither one improves your business stature or makes you more attractive to men.

10. Wear stockings, not socks, if you're wearing a skirt or dress.

Overdress

If you're not an executive, but you're looking to marry one, use this additional strategy. Dress up, so you appear to be a rung or two above your job level, but continue to dress in a friendly manner. If you're a clerk-typist, dress as an executive secretary would dress. If you're a secretary, dress as if you're a junior executive. If others confuse you with someone of a higher position, so much the better. You'll have better opportunities if you don't limit yourself by your appearance.

Even the lowliest file clerk can enhance her status by her accoutrements. A stylish hairdo, manicured hands, moderate makeup, or a small gold pin can stir a man into thinking that this woman is classy. He'll wonder what she'd be like outside the work environment.

Business Cards

Grandmother dropped her lace handkerchief in front of a young man and, if he was interested, he'd pick it up and they'd meet. If you dropped your handkerchief, you could be fined for littering. Times have changed, so you need a different strategy to meet men. Today, what you use is a business card.

When you meet someone who interests you, whether that interest is business or pleasure, give him your business card. You'll have business cards unless you are a probationary employee or the company views you as either negative or insignificant. After all, they even tag furniture and equipment.

Since your business card probably doesn't have your home phone number, have a separate set of cards for your private life. Give these cards to someone you know a little better. Some employers may object, because they don't want you to have a second job or your own business, or even your own business cards. But what you do off work is none of their business.

Use your business cards to open the door for you to start a conversation. They'll indicate there's a reason to chat other than animal magnetism. You'll be more comfortable if you can show a business purpose for meeting.

Name Tags and Badges

If you wear a uniform, you might be wearing a name tag or badge on your uniform. This name tag or badge can help you meet men, whether you are a waitress or a police officer.

If you have a choice as to the form of your name, avoid endearing nicknames such as Honey, Tootsie, or Angel. A stranger might not want to call you by such a familiar name, so he might not use any name in referring to you, or might avoid you altogether.

The shortened form of your name is fine, as long as it's readily recognizable. Use Suzy, Sandy, or Kathy, if you care more about friendliness than power. Use your full name if you care more about power.

Be sure your name is readily pronounceable, even if it's unusual. You want men to say your name and learn it by repeating it to themselves and out loud. They won't say your name if they can't pronounce it. If you do have a name that is difficult to pronounce, say it out loud and point out its uniqueness to start a conversation.

Voice

Your voice can be one of your best assets in meeting men at work. By changing your intonations, you can sound authoritative or friendly, as you choose.

Since you want respect as a professional or executive as well as attention as a woman, never speak in a singsong voice or sound squeaky. You don't have to diminish your authority to meet men, but recognize that a man is likely to be intimidated by your position. *Sound* friendly if you want him to think that you *are* friendly, or take the initiative to meet him.

In rare cases, you can use your authoritative tone of voice as a way of meeting men or arranging to see them after work, but don't emulate the female executive who said, "You, that's right, you over there. My biological clock is ticking."

DESIGNING YOUR OFFICE

Pictures

Your selection of photographs and paintings for your office can affect the way men perceive you and your chances of meeting the man of your choice at work.

If you want to show your interest in dating, use your office decorations. This doesn't mean hanging nude pictures of your favorite hunk on your office wall. These pictures may intimidate your male co-workers. Don't even put up pictures of men you're dating.

Be especially careful in hanging pictures with people in them. Do not have any pictures of an adult male unless it's blatantly apparent he is not your love interest. A man relates to a picture in a different way than a woman does. As a woman, if you come into a man's office and see a picture of another woman, whether or not the man is also in the picture, you would compare your attributes to hers and determine whether you have a chance with that man. If a man comes into your office and sees a picture of another man, whether or not you're in the picture, he'll assume you're taken. He feels you wouldn't display that man's picture unless you're committed to him, or at a minimum he's someone special in your life. The man in the picture may be your brother or someone you spoke to briefly on your last vacation, but the man in your office doesn't know this.

A picture with your children is a plus, especially if they

are active and healthy. It's a good conversation piece. Hang a picture of your six-year-old son tossing a football to you. Your visitor won't assume you're married if he sees pictures of you and the children without a man. Men also respond favorably to pictures of foreign places, cars, and planes.

Let your office decor tell the man something about you. If you have a boat, design your office motif to let him know it. A picture or a model of the boat can be a real plus. If your boss doesn't mind, leave a boating magazine on your desk.

Your Office

You're not an executive unless you have your own office. Don't let anyone tell you otherwise. Even then you might not be an executive. Your office should be large enough to meet with a number of people. After all, you might not want to be alone with a man you hardly know.

If you share an office, we're sorry to tell you that office sharing hurts your choices of finding love at work. In fact, office sharing has the disadvantages of a private office coupled with the disadvantages of working in an open area.

The presence of an office mate is intimidating to men. This is true whether your office mate is male or female. The man feels he needs a solid excuse to come into your office and chat with you if his conversations are subject to the scrutiny of one of your co-workers.

If your co-worker is female, your visitor will feel awkward in talking to you and avoiding her, but may have little to say to her. Also, he may feel that others are noticing the time he's spending in the office, so he'll have to use his time carefully.

If your co-worker is male, your visitor will view this fellow as your "office husband" and will feel that he's intruding in the other man's territory. Being in this office is worse than being in the bullpen because the office doors and walls present a barrier to all of your co-workers.

If you're sharing an office, ask to have your own office

or to join a semi-executive-level bullpen. Since office rules vary from one company to another, or even within a company, going back to the bullpen might not be a step backward in your career.

You may have to confide in your office mate before you go public with your relationship. If you can't change locations, but your office mate is an obstacle, you may be able to change office mates so you can find one who'll aid your quest.

Religious Symbols

Unless you're working for a church, religious symbols don't belong in your office. A positive and affirmative display of your religion may be viewed by others as an affront to theirs. These symbols will discourage men of different faiths from approaching you and may even dissuade men of the same faith who don't feel as strongly about it as you do.

Food for Thought

Keep candies on your desk if you don't have a sweet tooth. They'll provide one more opportunity for a man to visit. Jelly beans, peanuts, and hard candies are also tempting, but be sure you can resist them yourself.

Other Temptations

Items in your office may give a fellow an excuse to stop by. A full-length mirror may lure him to check his appearance before he meets an important client. Hang it high enough for him to see his face. An unusual or large calendar invites him to stick his head in the door. Calendars that have a word per day or a thought per day also give an excuse to stop by and chat.

Even if your space is limited to a desk, you can still

keep a magazine on it that attracts men. In one of the
drawers keep supplies that are commonly needed, such as
tissues, matches, rulers, erasers, and highlighters. Keep the TV
listings, a weekend magazine, a weekend event bulletin, the
local football team's schedule, or the sports section of the
newspaper. There's no need to clutter your desk or office,
but a corner with a few of these attention getters can make
you popular.

Office Location

If you work near the bulletin board, coffee machines,
exit, or men's room, you're also increasing your probability
of meeting men.

Signal Your Approachability

If you have an office, do certain things that indicate it's
okay to talk to you. Lean back in your chair with your hands
behind your head, put on music, open your door fully, or sit
elsewhere than behind your desk. Arrive early or stay late
and socialize during that time that's not officially office
hours. Teach your co-workers to associate any of these
signals with your approachability.

MEETING THROUGH THE JOB

Meeting *through* the job can be even better than
meeting *on* the job, at least if you have the right kind of job.
Either way, it's easier for you to break the ice if there's a
business reason to start a conversation or sustain communications.

Your clients, customers, or co-workers may include
men you would like to date. Medical journalists interview
doctors. Doctors have patients who are advertising execu-

tives. Advertising executives meet retailers who are placing their ads. Retailers may have customers who are lawyers. Lawyers represent medical journalists. These interactions—and others—may provide worthwhile dating opportunities.

Here are a few strategies that women in ten different occupations have used successfully. They'll help you develop your own so you can get the social benefits you're seeking from your job.

Waitress

One waitress spilled soda pop on a customer just to meet him. She fussed over the accident and offered to pay the bill. Then she gave him her address and telephone number, ostensibly so that he could contact her about the cleaning. He called her three days later.

A second waitress had a regular customer who liked pastry. She gave him a sample of the new pastries her restaurant was serving. Another waitress made sure to have hot coffee ready in advance for special customers she would see approaching the restaurant. Both are now doing well with men.

Nurse

A nurse switched from intensive care to private duty, selected her patients carefully, learned about their interests, and made herself indispensable to them. One patient was an investor, so the nurse read stock reports to him. Another patient was a lawyer, so the nurse kept him informed about new court cases. Last we heard, she was dating both of them.

Reporter

A reporter set up a church bulletin so she could get to know the minister. Then she interviewed the parishioners for the bulletin, making herself indispensable to the church and the minister. She's now dating the minister.

Prison Guard

Frieda was unhappy because she was not succeeding with men. When her town started sending traffic offenders to jail, she became their personal guard. No other women were in the vicinity, and Frieda became popular with the inmates. This newfound popularity lifted her spirits and self-confidence. She began dating many men and eventually married a prison administrator.

TV Journalist

An investigative reporter for a TV station in a medium-size city had frequent contact with the police. She spent a great deal of time with the media liaison for the police department, whom she eventually married. She's now the evening news anchor and he's the deputy police chief.

Lawyer

A lawyer began dating a judge she met in court. Once their relationship became serious, he couldn't continue to hear cases in which she was one of the attorneys, but they were able to see each other inside the courthouse as well as elsewhere as their relationship grew.

In our situation, Margaret practiced matrimonial law and international law while Bob practiced tax law and international law. We used our mutual interest in international law as one of the building blocks of our relationship.

Another lawyer wanted children but was facing the biological clock. She was discouraged in her social dealings with male lawyers because they put their careers first, ahead of their families and their wives' career. She married her male secretary, who was about ten years her junior.

Barber

A barber had been cutting her customer's hair every other Saturday for a year. When he missed one haircut, she wasn't concerned, but when he didn't show two weeks later, she became upset. She asked his friends about him and discovered he was in the hospital for an operation. When she visited him, she saw that his hair looked shaggy and offered to trim it while he was still in the hospital. Then she offered to give him a shave every two or three days, noting that he had limited arm movement because of the operation. He was released from the hospital a few weeks later and they married the following year.

Talk-Show Host/Teacher

She was a speech teacher and her husband was a corporate executive, but she gave up her teaching career when he was transferred to a small city. After they relocated, her husband died. Sometime later, the local radio station was looking for a talk-show host and she was hired. Within a few years, she was well known and well regarded in her listening area. She then created a series of in-company courses for a number of local businesses, teaching their executives the skills of public speaking. She's now dating a number of corporate executives she met through these courses.

Stewardess

A stewardess was attending college part time. On one of her flights from London to Sydney, she struck up a conversation with a graduate student from Australia who was studying in Britain. When she mentioned that she needed to use a library to complete research for her university degree, he offered to get her access to libraries in London and Sydney. He then asked her to get him a book that was available only in North America. She brought him the book, he took her to the libraries, and they married a few years later.

Highway Patrolman

A highway patrol officer monitored the CB radio channels to overhear truckers' conversations. Then her assignment was expanded, and she began chatting with drivers to find out more about their vehicles and cargo. During the course of this investigation, she developed a rapport with a few drivers who didn't know she was a police officer. Later, when one driver was coming into town, he invited her to join him for dinner at the truck stop. He was quite startled when this officer appeared in uniform and asked for him by name, but he got over the shock and they were married later that year.

STRATEGIES

Here are some specific strategies you can use to meet men through your job.

Conferences

If you're attending a conference or convention, wear your name tag during the sessions and even during the breaks. Put the name tag near your right shoulder, not your left, so that people can see it when they shake hands with you.

Greeting Strangers

Since you can't get an "I do" without a "hello," you need to know how to meet and greet strangers you meet at work.

Your greeting strategy depends on your job. If you're a receptionist, you should view yourself as a professional greeter. Display this attitude even if greeting people is just part of your job.

If you're making sales calls, you're on the opposite side of the fence. Your business success and personal happiness may depend on the way in which you impress the person who is greeting you. The key is to be both friendly and memorable.

Customers

Make a friendly overture to your customers by suggesting the first appointment of the day. Let him know that if he arrives a half hour early, he can join you for morning donuts and coffee. If you want to indicate even more interest, suggest an appointment near lunch or dinner and offer to introduce him to the great Italian restaurant right around the corner. Let him know that you'd enjoy his company for a social occasion.

Work-Related Publications

If you pay dues to a work related organization that has a newsletter or other publication, urge this publication to include social events of interest to members. In fact, it could be an ideal publication for a personal ad.

CHAPTER 7
Building the Relationship

You have access to men as never before. You can meet any businessman, whether he works for your company or a competitor, is a supplier or a customer, or is a provider of services to your company. You can meet him at a convention, conference, or tradeshow, or when you're doing a feasibility study or submitting a bid proposal.

When you meet him, treat him as a colleague. Introduce yourself, give him your card, and if you wish, suggest a subsequent get-together. Seize these opportunities for business and romance. You have plenty of reasons to make the first move, so don't wait to be asked.

MEETING AND PURSUING YOUR COLLEAGUES

Company Goals and Personal Goals

Even a company that frowns upon love at work expects its employees to be friendly and cooperative. Use this company goal for your own purpose, to build a romantic relationship. You have access to everyone around you. Since you're working with them, you're close to them both mentally and physically. Your co-workers become your captive audience. This group may include your ideal mate. If you conduct your quest in accord with company policy, you may get a promotion as well.

Overcoming Male Fears

A man may be uncomfortable if you make a sexual advance, or even if you suggest a social get-together with him, especially if you're the first female executive who approaches him. He fears that such an encounter would be devastating to him, and that he is in a no-win situation. He revives his teenage feelings of inferiority, and focuses on his physical imperfections. He views himself as an unattractive middle-age man. From his standpoint, he is growing older, not better.

The male executive doesn't believe that you're really interested in him as a man and convinces himself that you're interested in him because of his position in the company. He also fears blackmail, especially if the relationship is forbidden by the company. He is afraid to take the risk. He attributes his reluctance to good judgment, but his sense of inferiority is the key factor.

You can overcome his fears by taking the initiative for friendship, by not making a sexual advance. Don't let your words or the general ambiance of your get-together bring up the issue of his sexual desirability. Instead, treat him as your mentor, and ask for advice, not favoritism.

Meeting Men

Learn who's who. If you start by learning the names of the men around you or who cross paths with you in the lunchroom, in elevators, at break time, or meetings, you're on your way to finding a great mate. Don't focus only on the men and ignore the women or you'll be labeled a flirt. Get to know your female co-workers and network with women who are interested in meeting men. Later, you can introduce each other to available male friends or relatives.

The male executive you are looking to meet views himself as his own little planet, the center of his universe, and generating his own field of gravity. If you recognize and respect his importance, he'll be willing to meet you. One approach is to meet him on his terms by letting him know that he has interesting ideas, a wealth of experience, or a different slant on things. Alternatively, you can challenge him on first meeting. "So you're the man who discontinued our most profitable product," "Did you really think there is a market for milk and orange juice blended together?" or "What did happen to our investment portfolio?" The one thing you can't be is boring.

Getting to Know Him

Don't trust an important decision, such as your choice of future mate, exclusively to your sense of sight. As long as a male colleague doesn't completely turn you off physically, invest some time in getting to know him. Take a few minutes or more each day to learn about the men with whom you're in contact.

Often you can't break the ice directly when you're interested in a colleague, but you can gradually chip away the ice. Take the initiative, but do so gradually and cautiously while remaining businesslike.

Talking to Him

Greet each man by name. It's his favorite word. Then say something that lets him know you recognize his individuality. For example, if you know he is building a vacation home that he works on every weekend, ask about his progress. The fact that you care enough to remember his personal life is going to make an impact on him. Give him a few minutes of your listening time.

If you can, get to know every man you encounter through your job. Make sure he knows you well enough that he recognizes you, greets you with a warm hello, and reacts favorably to you. Men talk to each other and discuss the women in the workplace. It's to your advantage that when men talk about you, they say that you're friendly and happy. A newly available man is likely to come over to meet you. Your male colleagues may be your greatest press agents.

When you're strongly attracted to someone, you often worry about what to say after "hello," but men agonize even more than you do. Make conversation easy for him by talking about work.

Once you've met a man who interests you, find out more about him. Ask him questions about himself, check with the corporate grapevine, and be observant when you're in his office. At a minimum, you need to know what he does in his company, his general reputation at work, his marital status, and a few other personal facts.

Find out more about the man by asking him about himself. Ask him about his past and his future, and then listen to his answers. Avoid asking him detailed questions about his work until you know him better, but he'll eventually talk about the present.

Using the Grapevine

The tidbits you pick up from the corporate grapevine can save you a great deal of time and effort, especially when a man claims to be eligible but isn't. However, the grapevine will give you some information that is erroneous, misleading, or both because it transmits certain behavior patterns inaccurately.

When you check up on him, remember that the corporate grapevine works in two directions, so your inquiry may get back to him. You don't know who's loyal to him and will tell him or lie for him. Also, you may appear nosy and may be putting your contacts on the spot if they have confidential personnel or payroll information.

Getting to Know Him

If a man is available and interesting, and the relationship continues to grow, find out as much as you can about him. Target your conversations to uncover attitudes toward work and other aspects of his life. Ask him why he likes or dislikes a certain person, place, or event.

If you're working closely with someone, you may think you have more in common than you actually do. Don't rush into the relationship. Take the time to be sure you really have a great deal in common.

Since you're busy at work and can invest only moments a day in these conversations, check out his most important values first to make sure they aren't in conflict with yours. Even if you learn only a fact each day about someone, it still won't take too long before you have enough information to know if he's a potential mate or not.

Using His Passion for Work

A man has many passions that are unrelated to sex and love. His next greatest passion is likely to be his enthusiasm for work. When you're in contact with him through work, you're aware of his work activity and his emotional investment in his occupation. It's easy and natural for him to talk about this successes with you, and even his failures. If you encourage him to talk about the highlights of his day, he'll tell you about his accomplishments and associate you with those positive emotions. The more he speaks with you and shares these passions, the deeper the feelings he invests in you. If you listen long enough, you could get him to fall in love with you even if you've never had a romantic conversation with him.

Don't be concerned when he talks about the negative happenings of his day. The end result of telling you his woes is a feeling of relief he'll come to associate with you. You'll be in a favorable position compared with other women because you'll be there on the job with him, seeing, feeling, and reliving his life with him.

Praise

Every man wants praise, especially in the workplace. Praise him where you can, but never build him up at your expense. If you want him, let him know he is special enough for you.

If you praise him in front of your colleagues, no one can accuse you of doing anything improper. You haven't batted your eyelids, just acted friendly and social, and strictly in line with company policy. By the time he invites you out, you should know whether you want a more personal relationship with him.

Criticism

If praise doesn't work and he's not showing any interest in you, try criticism. But, remember that what you say will get back to his friends.

Keep the criticism personal. Tell him his suit would look better if he got one in his size or tell him he needs a haircut. Don't criticize his race, religion, national origin, job, neighborhood, or school. His colleagues may have the same background or job or school. If they hear your comments through the grapevine, they'll be offended by a comment that could also apply to them.

If the criticism is personal, and he mentions it back to his male colleagues, they'll reemphasize your comments, not defend him, since men are not usually supportive of each other in this situation. If you told him that his suit would look better if he got one in his size, and he tells his buddies, they'll tell him that his suit wouldn't look good no matter what size it was.

Boosting His Ego

Your fellow has to work for a living, please his boss,

compete with his co-workers for clients and promotions, and take guff from the public. There are many days when he needs an empathetic ear, a pat on the back, and a reminder that he is special and not just a cog in the wheel.

You're in the perfect position to know when those moments occur and be there to boost his downtrodden ego. You could become indispensable to him. What a great position to be in if you want him as a mate.

Be sure to boost him up without pulling yourself down. Let him know that he's superior to other men, but not superior to you.

Disagreements

When people are in total agreement, they usually have little to say about the subject. Agreement doesn't lead to continuing conversation. On the other hand, if disagreements are too strong and strident, a relationship is not possible over the long term.

How much disagreement facilitates conversation and keeps people out of boredom without being so severe that this disagreement weakens the relationship? An appropriate level of disagreement is about five percent. For example, both you and he should basically agree about your preferences for recreation. Your choices and his should be pleasing to both of you, but there are likely to be a few things that one of you likes and the other doesn't. Find out about these disagreements before the relationship becomes too serious.

Proximity and Curiosity

When a man sees you continuously, it's only natural for him to become sexually curious about you, even if he wasn't particularly attracted to you in the first place. The longer you're in the man's sight, the more his curiosity builds up if there's even a glimmer of hope that it would ever be satisfied. An outsider could spark his curiosity, but all other factors being equal, he thinks about you. Your proximity to him may be providing you with a similar impetus.

Be Selective

You've been saying "hello" to everyone you meet through your job or on your job, and you're not aloof or snobbish, but dating is another story. Don't go out with everyone. It's easy to be selective because you're not in an all-or-nothing situation. When a man shows interest in you, you can get to know him gradually in the work environment and then through work-related socializing before you go out with him. If you might be interested, but you aren't sure yet, delay the date rather than turn him down.

Men will like you better because you're selective. Each man believes he's special. You add to his sense of uniqueness if you select him and not others. You're letting him know that he impressed you.

Be more selective in the work context than elsewhere, because each man you date will see the others and be faced with the reality of whom you're dating. Also, it might weaken his courage to invest emotions in you. If you've loved and left too many in the workplace, he may worry that he'll meet the same fate.

OVERCOMING HIS SHYNESS

At work, a man has little courage to approach a woman he likes, but he might have even less courage to approach a woman outside work. At work, he sees you often enough to build up a sense of familiarity. He loiters near you in hopes that you'll speak to him. You get several opportunities to meet him at work, but away from work there's only a brief chance to talk and he usually passes it by.

Other men are even less courageous at work than they are socially. A man may be especially reluctant to approach you at work because he's more concerned that you'll reject him or he's worried that the rejection will be more painful. Here are ten possible reasons why he's so shy:

1. He's reluctant to approach any woman because he fears that he'll be rejected and that this rejection will become public knowledge. He's especially sensitive about approaching a woman at work. Then, if she rejects him, he knows he's going to get a lot of ribbing from his pals.

2. When he's away from work, he can convince others that he's more important than he really is. Since they don't know him, he can create a favorable image. He'll manipulate and even exaggerate, but he believes that the right woman won't hold it against him. His attitudes are like those of a woman who wears a padded bra and expects the man to overlook the shortage.

3. If he tells his buddies at work that he's interested in a female co-worker, they'll try to convince him he's out of her league. They'll discourage him to save him from embarrassment. With cheerleaders such as these, the guy loses what courage he did have.

4. If he's turned down, he fears his male supervisors will think he's not much of a man, and he worries that they'll start finding fault with his work or treat him with less respect. If you turn him down, he fears he could lose his job. His fear may not be *realistic*, but it is *real*.

5. In his own mind, he is surrounded by overwhelming competition at work. Let's assume that his department includes his boss and five other men. His self-evaluation process may go something like this when he contemplates his chances with you:

   A. I don't have as much power or money as the boss.
   B. I'm not as tall or as handsome as Carl.
   C. I'm not as young as Ted or as much of a stud as he is.

D. I'm not as educated or as well spoken as Tom.
E. I have the baldest head of any man here.
F. The new trainee drives a better car than I do.

By the time he compares himself so unfavorably to all the other men, he convinces himself that you couldn't possibly be interested in him.

6. If he goofs on the job, and his boss yells at him, everyone knows it, including you. He's afraid that events which are beyond his control will diminish him in your eyes.

7. If awards are given for job performance and he's passed by, you'll know that others are doing better work. He worries that you'll reject him once you know how the company evaluates his work.

8. He's aware of the disadvantages of your seeing him as he really is. He lacks the mystique a stranger could have. You can learn unfavorable facts about him through work. Maybe his ne'er-do-well brother comes by the job site asking him for money, maybe his family squabbles tie up the phone lines, maybe he's behind on a payment and a creditor is pestering him, or maybe his parents speak broken English. Any one of these situations could embarrass a man who's trying to impress you with his superiority and desirability.

9. He may have an impressive wardrobe for dating, but he's not wearing it when he's with you. Because of his limited budget, his work outfits are unfashionable by comparison. You see him as he really is, not in the way he wants women to see him.

10. You'll notice his priorities, even toward money and food. Does he skip meals or buy food from a vending machine to save money, or does he put food ahead of other priorities? Is he social or shy, well mannered or rude, assertive or overwhelmed by others? He can't hide his attitudes and behavior patterns day in and day out, but he doesn't want to be this open with you until he knows you like him.

Beyond His Façade

When a man is socializing, he usually puts up a façade that hides his innermost feelings and thoughts. The real him is only known to the handful of people he chooses to be himself with. Often times he's afraid that a women will reject him if she finds out that he isn't the highest man on the totem pole socially, professionally, financially, or in other ways he thinks are important. He may exaggerate his importance and what he does, but if he's bragged too much, he knows he can't live up to the image of himself he's created. He avoids future meetings with the woman if she hasn't been dazzled by his personality in a few dates. He knows he can't keep up the façade much longer, so he tests her by not calling but hoping that she'll call him. She usually interprets his actions as a loss of interest in her and her pride keeps her from seeking him out.

Your Strategy

Now that you know what added fears he faces because he works with you, turn this knowledge to your advantage. Whenever you become aware of his sensitivity, remind him that he's special to you and that you need not be concerned that you'll feel any less affection for him. He'll enjoy knowing you like him despite the minor adversities he faces, and he'll love you all the more for it. Even go a step further and be his public relations person to his co-workers. Help him maintain a strong self-image in his world. This strategy will make you indispensable to him and his choice above all others.

IS SOMEONE INTERESTED?

If there are fifteen men working with you, the chances

are that at least one man is attracted to you. Could you spot the one in fifteen who really wants you? Probably not, because he usually isn't the guy who asks you out or even talks to you. He's terrified of the possibility you'll reject him. Your rejection would crush him so deeply that it's less painful for him to hope that someday your paths will cross and you'll notice him than it is for him to confront you with his desire for you.

He's not going to sit down and start a conversation with "Let me tell you about myself. I want you to know me, and know what life with me would be like." However, that's precisely what he'll be communicating by his actions.

Start to look around you to find that one man in fifteen. Focus on his behavior at work. Here are fifteen typical patterns that indicate interest:

1. He does his job conscientiously, in part because he hopes you'll recognize his superiority to other men and in part because he fears being too distracted by you.

2. He's solicitous of your needs at work. For example, he may hand you a package of new memo pads, a handful of pens, or a package of paper clips. If he does this for few people, or only for you, he could be the one.

3. He gives your work recognition when he talks to others and often indicates your superiority on the job.

4. Are you ready for this one! He may make it a point to talk to you about women in his life, in hopes that you'll be impressed with how others desire him. However, since these stories are just to impress you, you won't actually see him with these women in any really serious or romantic behavior.

5. He talks about his goals and where he expects to be ten years down the road, especially if he is now struggling for survival. He hopes to impress you by painting a rosy future.

6. He mentions what he owns and describes his present lifestyle. He talks about his home, his income, his hobbies, his weekends.

7. If he receives awards or any other recognition, he'll make sure you're aware of it.

8. He'll talk about his health, his family, and any obligations he can't readily set aside.

9. He reveals his personal philosophy or religious goals to you if they're uncompromisable principles to him.

10. He mentions his expectations about children and married life to apprise you of his ideas.

11. He tries to arrange physical proximity so you'll notice him.

12. He reveals his idiosyncrasies to you, whether they are his pet peeves or crucial causes.

13. He'll use the grapevine to gather information about you.

14. He'll seek a work assignment or project that will enable him to be with you.

15. If you and he are photographed together, he'll save the photo even if his only copy is from a newspaper or magazine and many others are in the same picture.

ASKING QUESTIONS

There's probably an ideal man for you in every hundred men you do business with. If one of your business contacts interests you, you can get to know him in a way that's a good business strategy as well as a good personal strategy.

The more you know about your contact's interests, the better you're able to know if you can—and want to—satisfy them. Ask him questions that concern your business relationship, but then ask questions that will open him up to talking about himself and his personal history. Your goal is to get him to talk about himself and to view you as an acquaintance beyond work. Here are twenty questions you can use:

1. What was his first job?

2. What is his favorite job? Least favorite job?

3. How did he get his present job?

4. What was the longest time he worked on one job? The shortest time he held a job?

5. Did he ever work in a uniform? Suit and tie?

6. Was he ever fired? Why? Did he fire anyone?

7. Did he ever work where women outnumbered men? What was his reaction?

8. Did he ever have a woman boss?

9. Did he ever work directly with the public? Did he like it?

10. What was his physically hardest job?

11. What was his toughest job?

12. What were the oddest hours he ever worked?

13. What was the most unusual moment at work? Most embarrassing moment?

14. Did he ever travel much on his job?

15. What's the most dangerous job he's had?

16. What does he expect to be doing in the future?

17. When does he expect to retire?

18. Does he ever think about going into business for himself?

19. Was he ever in a family business?

20. Would he want his children to follow in his footsteps?

CHANGING THE RELATIONSHIP FROM CO-WORKER TO LOVER

If He Turns You On But Doesn't Ask You Out

If your intriguing co-worker hasn't invited you out yet, continue asking him about himself. Then, right in the middle of a story you know he wants to relate, say you must dash back to your desk. Indicate that you'd love to hear the whole story, but it'll have to wait until after work or tomorrow. If he experiences a few frustrations in finishing his stories, it should occur to him to invite you to go someplace where you can talk in a leisurely manner. If it doesn't occur to him to invite you out, take the bull by the horns and say something like: "Larry, what you do to me is unfair! You have too much to say for the little time we have to talk. I'm inviting you to lunch next Monday. Maybe on a lunch hour I can get in a few complete episodes from the life of Larry."

Be cautious about asking a man out. If you do, invite him for a business event, not a social get-together. Some men still don't like being asked out on a date. They want to believe they discovered you, instead of the other way around. Break the ice, not his ego.

When he does invite you, and you want to see him again, accept his invitation promptly. Sound gracious, but not grateful.

HOW TO TELL HIM YOU LIKE HIM

It's impractical to blurt out your affections, especially on the job. Instead, use strategies which progress slowly in that direction. Then you won't scare him off or make a fool of yourself. Start with general conversations, but move to personal conversations and then to intimate conversations as the relationship develops. This plan should take three weeks:

Week 1

Start with general conversations that include greetings, general remarks about the weather, impersonal questions or comments, statements that are part of your job, and things you would say to anyone. Say something to him that lets him know you're aware of his presence. Comment on his cheerful hello or pleasant smile. Tell him that you like his tie, hairstyle, or outfit, or hint that he looks like a dashing character on TV. Follow up with a friendly "hello" the rest of the week, and as long as you continue to be interested in him.

Week 2

Ask questions that refer to personal facts about him, such as his family or job, but talk about things and events that are readily observable.

Use light criticisms as well as compliments. Tell him that his tie is crooked or not as attractive as his others, or his shoes need a shine, or his hair needs a trim.

Let him know that you dare criticize him because you like him so much you can be honest with him. Admit that you're attracted to him because he is quite special, not one of the ordinary men you work with. Tell him that you hope he won't be offended when you tell him how he can be even better.

He knows *you* must be special because you figured out that *he* is special. He feels that if you think that much about him and even speak up to correct his flaws, you must like him. In fact, you may be the woman his mother always told him would come along someday and recognize how special he is.

Week 3

Your conversation becomes intimate when you discuss his feelings and other things that are too private to be readily observable. Ask him as many "why" questions as he'll willingly answer.

DATING EXCLUSIVITY

If you're dating a co-worker, make him your only office date. Dating around can hurt your career because it gives others a chance to think that you're at the office to play, not to work. Of course, if the relationship ends, you can find someone else at work. If you're dating men you meet through your job rather than on your job, exclusivity isn't necessary, but discretion is.

SLEEPING YOUR WAY TO THE TOP

If you're writing advertising jingles, developing a tax strategy, or designing new packaging, you have a real chance to shine compared with your co-workers. But in sex you can't be that different or that much better.

Sleeping your way to the top usually doesn't work, but it sure beats sleeping your way to the bottom. People rarely get promoted because of their sexual activities.

LOVE AND MONEY

Career Attitudes

Before the relationship gets too serious, discover your prospective spouse's career attitudes. Even if the man you're planning to marry is actively pursuing his career, he may view marriage as an excuse for a change in career direction.

He may be looking forward to quitting the advertising agency, giving up commercial art, and becoming a sculptor. Or he may believe that both of you should quit work and travel around the world. Discover his goals before you make your wedding plans. Don't assume they're the same as yours.

If you're planning to continue your career after marriage but your spouse isn't, be aware of the risks. You'll be his meal ticket, but if your marriage ends he may claim that he gave up his career for you.

A marriage contract is essential if you're both working, especially if you're the type of people who have a will.

Don't Be a Gold Digger

Chances are, you never thought of being a gold digger, but in case you did, here's a warning. Don't use your job to catch a man and then up and quit work. Don't even think about it. It'll be quite an unpleasant surprise to a man who expects his wife to be his compatriot and co-insurer. Your unilateral decision to quit work will probably destroy the marriage.

Communication is essential. If you expect to give up your job once you marry, and he doesn't know this in advance, you may be in for a great deal of marital strife.

Even if the marriage doesn't end because family or religious pressure prevents its dissolution, the marriage will have gone sour. He'll feel trapped and exploited and will become despondent. You'd feel the same way if he stopped working and thought of you as his meal ticket.

Paying for the Date

Social behavior changes more slowly than business behavior. Even when the man and woman have equal pay, the man is likely to be paying for the date. There's an advantage to paying for the date because the person who pays has greater control over where to go.

Women who bear a greater percentage of dating costs are more popular with men because they make the men feel they're desired for themselves and not for what they can provide. Some men feel awkward in initiating a discussion of dating costs so it's easier if you raise this subject.

When you first start dating, the man invests one of two things—money or emotions. If you ask to be taken on costly dates, he expects that after spending enough, he will be rewarded with your sexual favors. Think of it this way: How much money would you spend to take a fellow out if all that you'd get for your money is the pleasure of his company? If he talked just about himself, and wasn't thinking of you and what you wanted to talk about, you'd be doubly annoyed because you've paid for his ego trip. Men are just as annoyed if they pay for the date and get nothing in return—not even their choice of conversation topics. Put yourself in that situation to realize what you can do to be a desirable date. You have an advantage over other women because you know his disposable income, and he need not pretend he has deep pockets if he doesn't.

Financial Strategies

Since you work together and you know his financial

status, be considerate. Use any or all of the following ten techniques, as a wife would do.

1. Offer a less expensive alternative. If he invites you to a fancy French restaurant, let him know you love Mexican food too and you know of a restaurant with great food and better prices.

2. If he insists on an expensive event, offer to supply the tickets for some future event.

3. Mention that the pleasure of dating him comes from being with him, so where you go is very secondary. Even fishing could be fun with him.

4. Take responsibility for some of the dating costs. When you invite him or suggest an activity, let him know he'll be your guest. Arrange with him beforehand how to handle costs in a manner not embarrassing to him. If he's overly sensitive, give him the money first so he pays or reimburse him when you get home.

5. Supply some of the miscellaneous costs, such as transportation, gas, long-distance telephone calls, the gift for the host of the party, the rental of his tuxedo for your sister's wedding, parking, and tipping.

6. If you have the same lunch hour, bring him lunch to help him save a few more dollars for dating.

7. Cook him dinner once in a while.

8. Brainstorm ideas that cost little to execute, such as riding through an area of beautiful homes, strolling on the shore, building a bookcase together, going to an enrichment class at night, or playing cards. Think of what you would do for amusement if you were married.

9. Offer to do things a wife would do, such as going with him to select his mom's gift for Mother's Day and helping him wrap it. If it's income tax time, help him fill out his tax forms.

10. Organize a small gathering for his friends at your place or at his. You want his friends to appreciate you and become advocates for your relationship.

Discuss finances openly with him. You know approximately what he earns. If you really can't afford to meet any dating costs, be honest about your lack of funds so he knows you're not rejecting him.

Dating has become an artificial mating ritual. You're brainwashed into believing that the purpose of a date is for you to be entertained. The forgotten purpose of dating was and is mate selection. If marriage is your goal, then use dates to lead you and your potential mate into behaving as a husband-and-wife team. Then it's easy to take the next step into marriage.

CHAPTER 8

Your Company and Your Co-workers

Some of your co-workers will wish you well in finding love at work, some couldn't care less, yet others will become angry and jealous. Let's see how your love relationship will interact with your work relationships and how you can make this interaction a positive one.

KEEPING YOUR PRIVATE LIFE PRIVATE

Once you find love at work, you'll have to decide whether you're going to keep it secret or go public. It takes planning and discipline to keep your relationship secret, but there are disadvantages to premature disclosure, so make your revelations carefully.

Some couples strive to keep their relationship secret because they fear they'll be punished for breaking company rules. Others fear gossip. If your employer opposes love at work and you're looking for love, treat your employer as an adversary and make your plans accordingly.

Keeping your romance secret until you're sure about your lover puts stress on the relationship itself. Even so, keeping your relationship "undercover" is the safest strategy until you know the relationship is likely to continue. Don't expose your personal life for a casual acquaintance or fling. You can't keep love a secret forever. The longer and stronger your relationship, the harder it is to keep it private.

Visibility

Relationships with your colleagues are more visible than you might realize. It's difficult if not impossible to keep your relationship totally private forever if you're dating a co-worker. Secrecy is difficult even if you're dating someone you met through your job. People who are romantically involved are often not aware that others know about their relationship, but others often notice the clues.

The two of you may be far more visible as a couple than each of you is individually. Your visibility is heightened if you work in different departments and would not normally have contact with each other in the work context, but you're together frequently. If you're a marketing manager for computer equipment, and he's a chemical engineer, why would you be in regular contact with him? Either you have a relationship or you're developing an advance weapons system under a super hush-hush military contract, or so your co-workers think. A secret project may threaten the ranking of your colleagues within the company, especially if they're excluded, but a relationship between the two of you won't generally be perceived as a challenge to their jobs. Since you'll be a subject of conversation, it's better to admit to the relationship eventually.

Other factors can affect your visibility. The more dissimilar the two of you are, the more visible you are as a couple. If you differ greatly in height, race, or age, you're more likely to be noticed by the people around you.

How to Avoid Detection

Your right to privacy is not absolute. Don't expect privacy if you're smooching at the watercooler or enjoying each other's passions in an unused office. Here are 25 guidelines to help you keep your office romance secret:

1. Stand at arm's length when you talk to each other.

2. Don't be alone with him where others can discover you. Have someone else along, or go in a group.

3. Avoid traditional sexist behavior patterns that could give you away. Since he doesn't open the door for women generally, don't let him open it for you.

4. Don't indicate in conversation that you two are ever alone together, and don't speak of your "intimate relationship," even in a nonsexual context.

5. Don't lock yourselves in his office or yours. Keep the door open—wide open.

6. Don't brush the lint or hair off each other's clothing unless you do that for everyone.

7. When you see him at work, have a project you could be looking at such as the budget for your division or a marketing proposal for your product line.

8. Have lunch with others as often as you have lunch with him and don't have long lunches together.

9. In vacation planning, travel on slightly different dates and to cities that are near each other rather than the same city, e.g., Minneapolis–St. Paul, Dallas–Ft. Worth, Ottawa-Hull, Edinburgh-Glasgow. Go to one while your lover goes to the other.

10. Don't come to work together unless you are part of a car pool and others are included.

11. Don't embrace on company premises, even on the

stairs or in the elevators, and don't sit on his lap in the office.

12. Don't spend too much time on the phone talking to him.

13. Don't be obvious about your affection, but don't go overboard in the other direction by avoiding any contact with him at work.

14. Don't call him by his private nickname.

15. Avoid long or frequent glances in each other's direction.

16. Use the same tone of voice when you speak to him as you do when you speak to others.

17. Watch your body language and avoid gestures that others could construe as sexual.

18. Unless you live near each other, don't be seen together when you're away from work.

19. Avoid joint business trips.

20. Don't make love during the middle of the day.

21. Don't start your own rumors. Keep his attributes to yourself.

22. The office is no place to give him your exclusive attention. Pay equal attention to all your co-workers.

23. Give your lover the privacy at work he needs to do a good job. If you keep popping up, you'll distract him and keep away those who need to see him.

24. Act as a team, not as a couple, because status as a "couple" implies "romance" to the public.

25. When you greet each other in public, shake hands. Avoid even the "friendly" kiss that is sometimes used as a greeting.

Watch Your Conversations and Body Language

Because you and your lover talk to teach other outside work, your conversations at work seem full of gaps to co-workers who overhear them. People usually have to set a background for the stories they tell. If the usual "stage settings" are missing in your conversations, the other participants in the conversation are likely to recognize that you are seeing each other after hours. People who spend a great deal of time together or share events complete each other's sentences. Now that you're aware that you're doing it, it's easy to stop.

Two people involved with each other tend to glance in each other's direction more frequently and look at each other longer when their eyes meet. The expression "You should have seen the way they looked at each other" indicates how human it is to communicate with looks. If you know that others are consciously or subconsciously observing your glances, you'll be more careful.

Making Partial Disclosure

You may enjoy fooling the company and hiding your relationship, but you're consuming too much energy hiding the relationship rather than nurturing it. Now it's time for the second phase of the relationship, partial disclosure.

You can't ignore the perceptions of your co-workers. Keeping an affair secret isn't advisable when there's a good chance your friends will figure it out and be angry if they aren't told.

Once a rumor starts because someone notices your glances or sees you together, admit interest in each other. If you can, indicate that what made you take notice of Sam in the first place was, in fact, the rumor that you were interested in him. Say: "Since I was accused of liking Sam, I decided to find out what he's like."

You can't keep your relationship a secret forever, but you can minimize the seriousness of the relationship. Tell your friendly co-workers: "Sam and I saw the best movie last Friday. You know, he's a wonderful person and fun to be with, but I don't feel serious about him." Admit to seeing him, but not to the depth of the relationship. Eventually, no one will believe it's merely friendship if you and Sam date each other exclusively and at every opportunity, but you do gain some time before you feel repercussions on the job. By that time, you and Sam may be the priority in each other's life, or willing to make the relationship secondary to work.

If you tell a friendly co-worker about your affair, and your employer objects to love at work, your friend could jeopardize your position at the company. If you have a bundle of money equal to a year's pay, is there a co-worker you would trust to hold it for you? Your job is as valuable as that bundle of cash, so select your confidants carefully.

Going Public

Now we come to the third phase in the relationship, full disclosure. If your relationship reaches such a point that others would have to be deaf, dumb, and blind not to suspect it, don't bother to hide it. In fact, the first person who should be told is your boss. The major fear a company has about closeness between two workers is a loss of loyalties to the company. If you apprise your employer of the romance, and that it's serious, you're being as up-front as possible.

Your close acquaintances could have hurt feelings because you didn't confide in them. Tell your co-workers that you didn't talk about your lover at work because you didn't want them to be burdened with the information. A co-worker may have felt a tug-of-war within himself between keeping your secret and revealing it to management. By keeping your co-workers ignorant of your affair, you've also kept them from that dilemma. Thank them for understanding your silence and tell them you'd want to be treated in the same way.

Overcoming Guilt

A couple that has a relationship at work might spend a great deal of effort keeping their relationship secret. Sometimes they do so because of their own need for privacy, not because they're violating company rules. Nevertheless, they hide from their co-workers as though they're doing something shameful and illegal. There's no need for guilt or shame unless you've really harmed the company by your romance. To compensate for any feelings of guilt, make sure the company gets even more loyalty and work from you than before. Giving your employer a little extra time or effort should set things right.

SEXUAL POLITICS

Pursuit of Power

Your romance alters your company's power structure because you and your lover will start making decisions jointly without input from others. Your collaboration means you'll have greater impact together than you have separately. Your co-workers don't care about the sexual aspects of your relationship, but are jealous because you've usurped power, whether power over finances, hiring, or product development. They worry that your lover will help your department get a higher budget or a sought-after project, or that you'll shift overhead charges from his department to theirs or arrange for him to get the choice new accounts. You'll face this problem even if you're not part of management. A woman photographer for a small newspaper works with four reporters, and she is in love with one. The other reporters question whether she is devoting adequate time and effort to assignments with them. You may have to demonstrate that you're together for love not power, which means allocating your time and attention in a fair manner.

Dealing with Staff Concerns

Your own staff may oppose your romance with another executive, especially if he's more senior. They'll think their chances for advancement are blocked because your attention is diverted and you won't move up. You may see open hostility, complaints to top management, and even blackmail if you're violating corporate rules. Your staff may think that you'll be dominated by your lover. If you can't dispel this fear, you'll lose control over your people.

If your boss is your lover and evaluates a number of employees, including you, the other employees at your level are even angrier than management because they feel that their own evaluations suffer. When you report to him, are evaluated by him, and get your raises from him, your colleagues may become irate. He'll have to demonstrate that work assignments and evaluations are truly objective, but that's not feasible in many situations.

Invisible Rules

If you want to succeed at love—and business—you've got to follow the invisible rules as well as the ones that are as plain as day. These rules are unwritten and often unconscious, but they fill the gaps between what's formally decreed and what actually takes place in business. Be attuned to these invisible rules if you expect to survive and thrive in the corporate environment.

Invisible rules have a major effect on relationships because people learn from prior incidents, such as when a man is fired for pursuing the boss's secretary or other employees are chastised for flirting near the watercooler.

Just as written rules differ widely from one company to another, so do invisible rules. Even if a company has few formal rules to directly dominate its employees, unwritten pressures can be just as intimidating. Learn the rules where you work or are considering working, but also learn how to challenge or circumvent these rules. Trying to obey every written and unwritten rule will only give you mental anguish and won't do the company any good either.

Power and Romance

Power and romance are often conflicting goals. Power is so important to some people that they seek a liaison at work as a means of increasing their power within the organization. They fall in love with power rather than a person. Others are so romantic that they put romance ahead of work, try to grab love where they can find it, and ignore the business consequences. You can avoid either of these extremes, but you need to establish your priorities.

Would you give up love if the company requires it or is love more important? Decide what you want and believe is possible before you become too deeply involved to be able to handle the situation. Base your decision on reality, not on what the rules ought to be.

Some people who do not date their co-workers make a conscious business decision not to do so. People who are highly career motivated may be wary of jeopardizing their advancement, or even their present position, by dating a co-worker. They're also unwilling to jeopardize their working relationships with others in the company. Work is their priority, and they don't want to take chances by becoming "involved." They're likely to verbalize their abstinence with a phrase such as "Don't play where you work."

You might not date a co-worker if you fear that the

relationship will fail and that others within the company will know about this failure. You may fear the embarrassment this could cause, or worry that your former heartthrob will disclose personal information about you to people within the company. This concern is legitimate, so take account of the man's reputation for being discreet before any indiscretions occur. Check him out before you check in.

The reality is that if you must separate work and play, you can't do both well and one is likely to fall by the wayside. Nowadays, that is likely to be the personal relationship.

AVOIDING FAVORITISM

One of the most common complaints about love at work is that the lovers favor each other in the workplace. These complainers do have a point, because favoritism can poison the work atmosphere for others. Favoritism can happen naturally as part of the showing of love and affection. However, it's usually possible to solve favoritism problems without destroying the relationship.

In extreme situations, a lover deliberately seeks work favors. Your lover may feel battered and bruised by the world, and may be seeking favoritism at work to boost his ego. Do massage his ego, but not at work.

Tell him he is superior to other men, but don't tell him that he's superior to you. Let him know that you think he is kinder, more intuitive, more logical, and more perceptive than his co-workers, but that you're prejudiced. It may not be feasible to tell him he is brighter or harder working or more ambitious than they are if you want to preserve your neutrality at work. Thus, even your off-hours ego boosting is limited when you work with your lover.

Some lovers seek office favors. They'll flaunt their relationship and the power it brings. While men sometimes seek favoritism for reasons of ego, women are more likely to seek favoritism for reasons of power.

You may become someone's favorite for a reason that

has no connection with love or sex. Perhaps you enjoy the same sports, share common values and attitudes, belong to the same ethnic group, attended the same school, have the same religion, or come from the same neighborhood. Nevertheless, the favoritism problems are equally serious.

If people believe you're benefiting from favoritism, this perception can harm your career. You may be doing excellent work and receiving high evaluations, but they'll be discounted if people think you are going to bed with the person doing the evaluating. If you are dating your boss, your co-workers will attribute your advancement to your relationship, not your abilities.

The solution to the favoritism problem is to establish objective standards and then apply these standards. If you're the boss, let others know exactly how they're rated by you. If you're not the boss, try to surpass the standards so that the complainers will have no grounds for their complaints.

HOW MUCH DO YOU TELL YOUR LOVER?

You keep secrets from your co-workers, including secrets that pertain to compensation, technology, or marketing plans. But how do you keep secrets from a co-worker who's also your lover? You're more likely to tell secrets to your lover than to another co-worker because you're involved emotionally and sexually.

What you'll reveal to your lover depends on your personal standards, your attitudes toward the business, and your relationship with your lover. Many couples keep business secrets because they separate love and business conduct. Other couples tell secrets to help their lover to get ahead.

If you and your lover share information and business plans and talk about your co-workers, they'll feel uncomfortable. However, only a small portion of business should be so confidential that it's kept from employees within the same company. Choose a department in which information sharing is advantageous if you want to maintain your love-at-work relationship.

MANAGEMENT AWKWARDNESS

Managers generally ignore love at work because they don't know how to handle it. They're embarrassed to talk to their subordinates—male or female—about their personal lives. Male managers are especially uncomfortable discussing relationships because they involve emotional issues and other topics with which they're not familiar. Female managers are more comfortable with these issues but rarely have the authority to deal with them.

CONFLICT OF INTEREST

If you're dating someone you know on your job, or someone you meet through your job, you might be accused of having a conflict of interest. These accusations are sometimes legitimate, but not always, and you should be able to defend yourself when you are unjustly accused.

By conflict of interest, we mean that the company would be impaired financially and that an outside entity (supplier, customer, competitor) would benefit from disclosure of information, or a biased decision, e.g., to purchase from a particular vendor.

The company may be concerned that employees in its purchasing department are becoming too friendly with certain vendors and are overpaying for what they buy, that members of its sales force are too close to its customers and are selling their products too cheaply, or that individuals with business or technical know-how might be revealing this know-how to the company's competitors.

A bank can legitimately be concerned about relationships between members of its loan committee and borrowers from the bank. A manufacturer may be concerned about ties between its purchasing agents and vendors to the company.

Singling out love relationships as a conflict of interest is inappropriate. If these rules apply to dating, they should apply to other friendships and blood relationships. What if you belong to the same club as the people you do business with? Must you drop the membership or the friendship?

If you and your lover together have a special access to the company's reports, financial records, business secrets, or money, the company has a right to do something about it such as transferring one of you elsewhere. You might even suggest it.

A number of companies try to limit or stop social contact between its employees and the company's suppliers, customers, or competitors. A company might go even further and attempt to limit off-work contact among its employees. These restrictions, called non-fraternization rules, shouldn't be limited to dating, love, and sex.

A company can have different rules for different categories of employees. Employees who have contacts with vendors or customers or access to cash, personnel records, or business secrets can more readily be subject to these rules. The more people included in the rule, the less justifiable it is. Also, dating a co-worker should not be treated more harshly than dating a competitor.

You might belong to a professional society that says you must avoid any conflict of interest. The establishment—that's them—then tells you that you must avoid even the appearance of a conflict of interest. Such a rule may be overreaching, especially if dating and marriage are singled out, or if other relationships are exempted from this ban.

Intramural Rivalries

Intramural rivalries are commonplace in big business. Different divisions of the same company may be competing against each other for corporate resources, including advertising budget and computer time. This competition may become so fierce that each division comes to view the other as the enemy. If you and your lover work for rival divisions of the company, your relationship may be affected.

The specter of disloyalty may be raised. Some executives assume the woman will put her relationship first and her division second and will accuse her of disloyalty. Other executives will cast a jaundiced eye on the more junior of the two, but that also tends to be the woman. She may become the scapegoat for green toothpaste that didn't sell, a children's program that ran at midnight, or a tax strategy that backfired.

Do conflict-of-interest rules apply to these intramural rivalries? Suppose a company makes various competing products and employees are assigned to various product teams. Can your team leader object if your lover joins a competing team? Can the leader keep your lover off your team? What if your leader can do both? Then your lover is denied employment opportunities.

There can't be a conflict of interest if you and your lover work for the same company any more than there is a conflict of interest between the pitcher and catcher on a baseball team. Their skills and timing may differ, but these differences don't constitute a conflict of interest.

Avoiding Conflict of Interest

Don't accept the argument that you and your lover automatically have a conflict of interest within the corporation. In a sense, you're competing for scarce corporate resources, but all executives are competing and they don't have a conflict of interest.

If two lovers are granting each other business favors, the company can object because they're not doing their jobs properly. Job misconduct, not the nature of the relationship, is the relevant issue.

DEVELOPING PERSONAL STRATEGIES

Gossip

The company should punish gossipers instead of their victims, but companies rarely show such foresight. Try to diminish gossip by depriving the gossipers of information about you, but some gossip is unavoidable, no matter how private you are.

Your Behavior at Work

Imagine yourself taking a long plane trip. After the captain welcomes you aboard, he tells you a smooth trip is expected. You notice early in the flight that the copilot is a woman. Later, when the cockpit door opens, you catch glimpses of the pilot and the copilot smooching. Your flight attendant says, "Isn't it wonderful. Our pilots are in love." How safe would you feel in crowded skies, with unexpected turbulence or bad weather, if your pilot and copilot are distracted, even momentarily, by each other? You'd feel uneasy or worse.

The same concerns are relevant when you and your lover work for the same company, even if lives are not at stake. Unless you show as much seriousness as before, and it's wise to display even more, you'll make your bosses and co-workers uneasy about how useful you now are to the company. Here are ten guidelines to help you display as much effectiveness on the job as ever.

1. Maintain impartiality toward your co-workers.

2. Challenge your lover's ideas in brainstorming sessions and let him challenge yours. If you're both of one mind, the company needs only one of you.

3. If your lover talks to another woman, be friendly toward her. Jealousy makes you look out of control.

4. Keep secrets secret. If you break the confidence of even one co-worker, the others assume you'll do the same to them.

5. If you report to him, or he reports to you, ask to report to another at work, if feasible. At a minimum, keep written records of your evaluations and those of others in case your objectivity is ever challenged.

6. Be a bit freer in handing out compliments to co-workers. If you recognize their good work and let them know they're important to you, you'll turn around any negative thoughts.

7. Follow company rules whenever you can.

8. Dissuade gossip about others, so they in turn may dissuade gossip about you.

9. Be confident, since you're achieving both happiness and success. Act more mature, not younger, even though love makes you feel younger.

10. If you're aware of another office romance, mind your own business.

Dealing with Your Supervisor

Your private life is not any of the company's business, but you have to adhere to corporate rules or face the consequences. Your supervisor could be your first hurdle. These guidelines should help in dealing with your supervisor:

1. Listen carefully to your boss's comments on newspaper articles, current books, hot topics on talk shows, office events to get a feeling for his or her values. If you discover these views, you'll know how to present your relationship in the most acceptable way.

2. Even if the company accepts love at work, ask your supervisor to let you know if there's a conflict of interest.

3. If your boss starts complaining about your work and the only difference is that you're now dating a co-worker, your company is showing its disapproval of your relationship. Worse yet, it may be building up a complaint file so it can dispose of you. Try to narrow criticisms to specifics about your work so that you can defend yourself.

Other Strategies

1. The worst of all worlds is to look like the office flirt and not have a relationship. Be discreet.

2. Watch out for the old double standard.

3. Ask the participants of other romantic liaisons at work how they're treated and find out who are the supporters of love at work. Then join with them and form a support group.

4. Plan for career advancement conflicts. Nurture each other's career rather than stand in each other's way.

Displaying Happiness

Love can be joyous, even exhilarating, but be careful in displaying your happiness at work. Even if your company has a positive attitude toward love at work, it may draw the line at overt displays of affection.

You may be much happier than the people you work with—and you should be when you are in love—but don't let them see how happy you are. If your co-workers believe that you are having more fun than they are, it's possible they'll say things about you or do things to you that are harmful. They'll reflect on their own personal situations and start resenting you. Then they may start thinking you're underworked or overpaid. No one wants to pay you to have fun.

Making Your Co-workers Your Allies

Jealousy is a strong passion that can incite anger. If you can help your co-workers dissipate their jealousy toward you, you can turn them into allies. Take these precautions:

- Let them vent angers. If you sense hostility, make a statement such as "I hope I've done nothing to anger you—I value your friendship," or "We've enjoyed such a good working relationship, has something upset this?" Even if there's no response, your concern for their feelings takes the sharp edges off their hostility.

- If you're rewarded by a promotion or pay increase that your co-workers will discover anyway, brag a bit about why you deserved it. Discuss lightly, but without hesitation, the reasons for your success. If you don't, your co-workers may attribute your success to favoritism.

- Think of your co-workers and yourself as teammates. When you receive rewards or recognition, share the limelight. Speak of the great support you get from your fellow workers. If they're sharing the limelight with you, there's less chance they'll throw stones.

- If you move up, try to promote your co-workers who deserve it. If you get more power, use it to help them too. You're not going to stop people from talking about you, so give them good things to say.

Being Accessible

Are you and your lover always a couple even when you're at work? Do you come in to work together, spend much of your workday together, and have lunch together? If so, you're functioning more as a couple and less as a team than you should be. If someone can't have lunch with you but not your lover, or with your lover but not you because you are inseparable, you're losing effectiveness at work. Keep yourself accessible to others.

CORPORATE CUPID

Employers can play a positive role in bringing their employees together. Many companies play the role of Cupid, but not deliberately. Some companies sponsor bowling teams, picnics, and other events, and provide recreational facilities. These events and facilities encourage employees to meet, and some of these encounters lead to love and marriage. You may be reluctant to ask your employer or prospective employer whether it has events and activities that will help you find the man of your choice, but you can ask whether it sponsors activities that promote corporate teamwork.

Employees who marry respond with positive emotions toward a company that facilitates their relationship. The company can weave itself into the emotional and economic bond that the couple is building. Help your company see that it can benefit from love at work.

═══ CHAPTER 9 ═══
Overcoming Obstacles

If it were easy to find love at work, you would have already done so. Since good things usually don't come easily, you may be encountering obstacles in using your career to find your ideal mate.

BUSINESS AND PLEASURE

We grew up in a simpler world, where advice was dispensed in one-sentence dosages. Somewhere between pablum and milk of magnesia, we learned to "look before we leap," but we also learned that "haste makes waste." Yet advice concerning love and work was unambiguous: "Don't mix business and pleasure." No one bothered to tell us why, as if no explanation were necessary. We didn't know if mixing the two destroyed business and left the romance intact, turned romance into business, destroyed the romance, or ruined both business and pleasure.

The opponents of love at work may believe that corporate life is supposed to be distinct from family life, that personal relationships are anathema to business, or that business functions best when personal relations and emotions are minimized. You've already seen the harm that these attitudes are causing for millions of women, but it's easier to refute their ideas than it is to overcome them.

STRATEGY

To discover the solutions start with yourself and draw four concentric circles. Begin with the closest concentric circle, your personal attitudes that may be keeping you from finding happiness with one of your co-workers. We call these attitudes *the corporate incest taboo*. Then move outward to the next concentric circle, *peer pressures that may be stifling your opportunities for love at work.* Continue to move outward to the third concentric circle, *company rules against dating and marrying your co-workers.* Finally, you reach the fourth concentric circle, *government edicts against sexual harassment* that make certain normal dating activities illegal at work.

THE CORPORATE INCEST TABOO

Some people who are looking to date and mate limit their opportunities because they feel that their co-workers are off-limits. As a matter of personal policy, they won't date a co-worker, even if the co-worker is desirable and available.

If they're asked why they don't date someone they meet at work, they might not have a specific answer. They may just reply that they feel that it's "wrong." Or they may respond that they don't play where they work. They feel that dating a co-worker is improper because it's like dating a close relative.

The Incest Taboo

The incest taboo bars romantic emotions toward members of our immediate family, those persons we are closest to and know best. We're taught to feel guilty for merely having, even without expressing, such feelings of attraction.

For some of us, the workplace is the substitute family. We may even view our boss as a parent and our co-workers as siblings. No wonder, then, that some of us extend the incest taboo to the people we encounter at work and create a corporate incest taboo. We create this psychological fantasy in our quest for roots.

The family incest taboo serves many important purposes, especially as a barrier against transmission of genetic disorders where both parents have the same recessive gene. Obviously, the corporate incest taboo serves no such biological purpose.

Whom the Taboo Affects

People who have been at their jobs for many years or expect to remain with their present employers over the long term are most likely to accept the corporation as a substitute family and feel that there is a corporate incest taboo.

Of course, many of us do not draw this analogy between the workplace and the family, and if we don't hold such a view, we're much less likely to feel a corporate incest taboo. We're less likely to make this analogy if we view our job as temporary or as a stepping-stone to another position or to our own business.

The conventional incest taboo extends to parents, children, and siblings, as well as aunts and uncles. The taboo generally applies to first cousins, but usually not to second cousins. The extent of the corporate incest taboo is much less certain, but there are analogous limits. The taboo may apply to an employee's department or other work group, to persons in the company with whom the employee has business contact, or to the branch or division of the company in which the employee works, but the taboo is less likely to apply to the company as a whole. In extreme cases, someone might even feel that the taboo applies to their entire industry.

Overcoming the Taboo

You can sometimes overcome the corporate incest taboo by changing departments or changing jobs. If you meet someone you like, and the incest taboo is stopping him from dating you, your best strategy may be to put some distance between the two of you at work to prevent the incest taboo from operating.

A better strategy is to overcome the incest taboo by establishing a good working relationship and a friendship and easing into the dating relationship gradually. Even more important, develop closer ties with your real family, which will help you recognize that your co-workers are *not* your family after all.

PEER PRESSURE IN THE WORKPLACE

Peer pressures hinder your quest for love at work. You've left school and joined the work force, but you haven't left cliques behind. Both men and women are likely to become members of peer groups at work.

Gender-Based Cliques

Most men and women gravitate naturally to gender-based cliques. Male groups talk about sports and women while female groups talk about food and clothing as well as relationships. In neither case is the clique based on work roles. Gender-based cliques had more justification in the past when men and women had different job levels, but they persist today, especially among nonprofessionals. In fact, these cliques are usually divided by race and ethnic group as well as gender.

Negative Effects

Gender-based cliques make it harder for you to meet men at work. These peer groups reinforce sexual stereo-types through development of a "sour grapes" attitude.

Let's see what really goes on inside an all-male clique as the men comment to each other about the women who pass by. If you could listen and observe their conversations, you might hear them deriding both their female acquaintances and women they've seen but never met. A man who fears rejection from a woman is likely to express negative feelings about her looks or other things about her. This defense mechanism saves him from his friends' embarrassing questions such as "If you like her so much, why don't you ask her out?" He lacks the courage to approach her, but he'd rather his friends believe that the fault is hers. He tells them that "She's not sexy enough."

Women are no better. When you hear women talking about their male co-workers, their comments are often negative. You'll hear complaints that their male co-workers are not "real men" or that the men are "coming on" to them. A woman makes these negative comments as a defense mechanism to explain her own unpopularity. Since married women are not supposed to be popular with men but single women are, the most negative cliques are groups of single women, especially single women who have reached an age where most women are married.

Better Peer Groups

Among managers, professionals, and other educated people, peer groups are likely to be androgynous, with both women and men as members. These peer groups are likely to be based on job function, such as creative, financial, or marketing, since people who work together play together. These groups do not spend their time talking about sports or fashions, but are probably concerned with work-related topics.

Because these peer groups include both men and women, negative sexual stereotypes are much less common. If you're looking for love at work, form your office bonds with people of both sexes.

What to Do

Evaluate your peer group—the people you hang around the watercooler with, the people you have lunch with, and the people you socialize with after work. Does your clique include men and women? Are there both singles and marrieds in the group? Even if you can't become part of a peer group that has men and women, you can join a peer group that has both singles and marrieds.

Monitor the conversations in your clique. If these conversations are predominantly negative, your first step should be to raise the consciousness of your group. Ask your friends why they have these negative feelings. Then help them see the positives. If their attitudes remain negative, change groups.

RULES AGAINST DATING AND MARRIAGE

Some companies prohibit dating between co-workers. Others let you date as long as you don't do anything extreme—such as getting married. Then, they force one of you to resign. Anti-marriage rules are more common than anti-dating rules, but you had better know about both before you start dating a co-worker.

How Companies Differ

There are major differences between companies. Some try to control every facet of your life. Others leave you free to do your own thing. These are the crucial work-environment issues your high school or college placement counselor never mentioned.

The public is not aware of how greatly one company differs from another when it comes to rules about personal relationships. Even job hunters are not aware of these differences. Our study of company policies found some that impose no restrictions. As one company indicated, "Our hiring policy is quite simple: The best talent available." In contrast, another company that is competing for the same employees has an anti-nepotism rule that prevents the hiring of an employee's immediate family, in-laws, first cousins, and even second cousins. You'd have to be an expert in geneology just to know whether you're eligible to work there.

Rules against dating and marriage are more common in some industries than others. Older corporations are more likely to restrict personal freedom, while newer businesses rarely try to restrict dating or marriage. Large businesses are more likely to have burdensome restrictions, whether these rules are written or just understood, but small organizations are usually less restrictive and more likely to allow husbands and wives to work together. Creative businesses, where individuals are hired for talent, are more likely to allow relationships between employees, but this flexibility is lacking where the work is routine.

Karen Misses the Bus

As recently as a decade ago, companies could arbitrarily interfere with love at work. Here's one such example.

Karen was living with her boyfriend, Norman, a bus driver in Omaha. Perhaps lured by the thrill of the not-so-open road, Karen decided that she too wanted to be an Omaha bus driver. The Omaha Transit Authority refused to hire her, pointing to a rule preventing them from hiring the spouse of an employee. The transit authority claimed that the rule applied to Norman and Karen even though they were unmarried.

Karen brought this dispute to court and lost. The judges upheld the no-spouse rule and let the Omaha Transit Authority deny her a job. She was subject to the rule even though she wasn't married. If the transit authority had hired Karen, Norman and Karen would have driven separate busses and one wouldn't have been supervising the other, so the no-spouse rule shouldn't have been applicable.

Karen missed her bus, but she would have been eligible to be a bus driver if she and Norman had broken up. This court decision weakened the family unit, but most recent cases have more favorable outcomes.

Congratulations, You're Fired

Will marriage ruin your career? It might, if you marry a co-worker and your employer has a no-spouse rule. Many companies refuse to hire an employee's spouse, and, if two employees marry, require one to resign or transfer.

No-spouse rules used to be upheld as management prerogatives, but this is no longer so. Fortunately, courts and legislatures are now limiting or overturning these rules, making it safer for you to find love at work. We'll show you how to develop your own strategy to deal with their rules. You may be able to challenge your company's rule and win, even where the company's rule looks fair. Or, you may be able to get around the rule.

Examining the No-Spouse Rule

Before you start dating your colleagues, you ought to know how anti-dating and no-spouse rules work, and how they can affect you. Your employer's no-spouse rule must meet various requirements. If it fails even one, you can have the rule thrown out. A company will win only if its rule provides adequate notice, has a limited impact, is nondiscriminatory, is necessary for its business, and is reasonable.

Adequate Notice

You can have your employer's no-spouse rule declared invalid if the company did not notify employees about the rule. The rule must be in writing and posted in a very visible place or included in your employee handbook. A rule in your supervisor's handbook isn't enough notice unless you have easy access to the handbook.

Limited Impact

You can have the rule disqualified unless the company shows that its impact is limited. Consider these four examples:

1. A large company can't be hurt by employing a married couple, so it can't require one spouse to quit, but a small employer can.

2. A company can sometimes keep a couple from working in the same department.

3. The company can prevent one of you from supervising the other.

4. The company can sometimes insist that spouses work different shifts to minimize the risk of family problems at work. In a company with just one shift, you may be out of luck.

Business Justification

You can have your employer's no-spouse rule thrown out if it isn't needed, but your employer can show a business necessity for the rule if it improves productivity, makes the workplace more efficient, or makes working conditions safer, and there are no other ways to accomplish those three goals.

If a close relationship can weaken a company's system of checks and balances or its security, the company has the right to protect itself. The company can prevent one spouse from evaluating or supervising the other, making out the spouse's payroll, deciding the spouse's promotions, or checking the debts of the spouse to the company.

When spouses work together, problems can arise in planning the same vacation time for both, sickness can keep both spouses home, and marital fights might be brought to work. Your employer will win if it proves that these problems are serious. It can use absence records that show its sick leave and vacation scheduling problems, and can use an "incident file" to show family fights in the workplace.

Is the Company Reasonable?

Transfer to another department is more acceptable than relocating to another facility, but relocation is more acceptable than termination. The company can offer you a transfer to another department or facility to overcome the problems of spouses working together, as long as the new workplace isn't too far away. A company that will let you transfer will usually win.

Is the Rule Applied Fairly?

The employer can't pick and choose who's going to be affected by the rule. It must apply the rule across the board, to management and labor alike. Otherwise, there really is no rule, or the rule is unnecessary, or you're entitled to be an exception.

A no-spouse rule may be invalid because it discriminates against women who are looking for jobs. If the workforce is predominantely male, more wives than husbands will be denied employment. A company that discriminated against women will be compounding the effects of its past discrimination by imposing its no-spouse rule.

Corporate rules against love and marriage are often illegal because they cause sex discrimination or discrimination based on marital status. The company can win only if it's absolutely necessary to keep the couple apart.

Strategy

You now have a good idea whether your employer's no-spouse rule or anti-dating rule is invalid. Reevaluate your personal situation and consider attacking the rule that is keeping you from happiness. Tell the company that it's time to change policy rather than explain it to the courts.

If the company's rule is valid, and you or your lover must leave, the company must give the two of you a choice. Here are a few alternatives for choosing who should leave: the person who can more easily find another job, the one who has been there a shorter time, the one who can commute more easily, or the one who might like to change careers. If you don't choose, the company can terminate the one with the least seniority unless that policy discriminates against women.

DATING AND SEXUAL HARASSMENT

Sexual harassment is a real problem and a serious one, but it is often difficult to tell where dating ends and sexual harassment begins. A recent Supreme Court case has expanded liability for sexual harassment and further blurred the distinction between dating and sexual harassment, making men even more leery of encounters with women they meet at work.

The Supreme Court Decision

A woman bank teller in Washington, D.C., claimed that she and her boss had had sexual relations for four years. After all those years, she claimed that this sexual activity amounted to rape. She never looked for another job even though there are many banking jobs in Washington, D.C. She never complained to the head of the bank or to any supervisor and never complained to any authority. In fact, she never complained to anyone until she started the suit. However, the Supreme Court believed her story.

A woman who charges her boyfriend with sexual harassment because he dumps her is diverting attention from true sexual harassment problems. A lover's later remorse about her romantic actions shouldn't let her claim sexual harassment after the fact. A man should not be legally liable for an office romance that has gone sour. The Supreme Court case will be causing problems for years to come.

What Is Sexual Harassment?

The purpose of the sexual harassment rule is to prevent sexual activity from being required as a condition of employment, but the scope of sexual harassment has been pushed beyond its basic and intended scope. Social invitations have been portrayed as sexual harassment, even when not made by a supervisor of the employee and even when not made in a threatening manner. At the present time, even pre-dating and dating activities such as flirting, sex talk, and even compliments to a woman about her appearance, may be considered sexual harassment. Some extremists even claim that dirty jokes or sexy pictures in the workplace constitute harassment.

The law against sexual harassment provides great benefits, but a few extreme cases and administrative rulings have been wrongly decided because they have come to include normal dating and pre-dating activities. You're having a hard time meeting the male co-workers because of the excessive gripings of these women when their romances soured.

A man who recognizes this risk becomes extremely cautious in dealing with female colleagues. He feels that if he does or says the wrong thing he can be accused of sexual harassment. He may have to follow a personnel code with so many restrictions that he is afraid to speak with you without his lawyer present. Taking the fear to an extreme, some men are more reluctant than ever to hire women.

Taking the Initiative

The laws are keeping thousands of women at home alone on Friday and Saturday nights. It's too dangerous for men to ask them out. They have to be more cautious than ever in making advances to women they work with.

Flirting is sometimes mistaken for platonic friendliness and dating opportunities are missed, but friendliness is sometimes mistaken for flirting and these women receive unwanted attention. A man sometimes fears responding to a flirtatious look or words because the woman can claim that she wasn't flirting, just being friendly. How is a man going to know your intentions unless you tell him, since there are no standard definitions of flirting.

You may have to become the aggressor at work. Invite the man to join you for lunch or the next coffee break. If there's a meeting after hours, ask him to ride with you or offer to pick him up in your car.

These are a few guidelines some men use to avoid sexual harassment problems:

- Avoid even the appearance of impropriety.

- Never date someone who reports to you, even indirectly.

- Take "no" for an answer.

- Avoid repeated invitations.

Men who follow these guidelines will take "no" for an answer and won't ask you out again. Don't say "no" unless you mean it.

Encourage your legislators to exclude dating from the scope of sexual harassment. Flirting and enticement should be defenses to harassment charges, and harassment claims should be barred if they're not brought promptly.

SOLVING PROBLEMS

You need to get out of your own way. These obstacles to love at work can be overcome. You can analyze your own situation, determine that the corporate incest taboo should not apply to you, and then start acting on your own decision. Once you see that peer groups can be positive rather than negative, you can help steer your present group in the right direction or change groups. Then you can challenge or avoid company rules against dating your colleagues, and learn how to initiate contact with men in ways that overcome their fears of sexual harassment charges.

Discovering the Company's Policy

Very few of us are willing to ask about company dating and marriage rules before we are hired. To do so earlier would create an image that you're not serious about your work and your career. Even after you're hired, you're afraid to ask this question, implicitly rejecting the concept that there's no harm in asking. Your personal contacts in the company can be a valuable source of information because they'll let you know about the company's unwritten rules.

But what you don't know can hurt you. Find out the company's policies toward relationships. Get a copy of the company's rules and regulations. Look for positives such as flex-time, childcare facilities, and recreational facilities. Look for negatives such as forced political contributions and mandatory charitable donations.

Find out whether the female executives are married. If they're married, they're likely to be married to colleagues. While a male executive usually isn't married to a colleague, especially if he's past fifty, a female executive usually marries a colleague if she marries anyone. This information lets you know what the company expects from you.

There's far more variation among small businesses than among large companies. Some small businesses facilitate recreational sex. Employees can use the company's boat, condo, or credit cards for personal fun. Other companies don't even have a coffee break. Know the company before you start work.

In your quest for love at work, you can abide by company dating and marriage rules, circumvent these rules, or try to work with your employer to update these rules to reflect the new business realities. The choice you make will have a profound impact on your own future and on the companies you work for.

What Your Employer Needs to Know

Let your employer know that love at work is good business, that opposition to corporate romance has many negatives, including these three:

- Many creative people, especially those who are single and heterosexual, will flee from a rigid environment that prevents them from dating and marrying.

- An anti-love policy may be illegal, and even if it isn't, it won't reach the real conflict-of-interest problems that the company faces.

- The employee may become an enemy and try to circumvent the rules.

Let your employer know that it can expect these benefits and others from love at work:

- It can retain husbands and wives in the same field, whether lawyers or truck drivers, who are likely to go into business for themselves if the company doesn't let them work together.

- The company can gain the positive feelings that people have for those who made the relationship possible.

- Lovers will be able to spend more time at work and be more productive.

- The company can preempt the unions in dealing with these issues.

Opportunities for Labor Unions

Unions are actively fighting for employee rights in the workplace by challenging company rules that restrict dating or marriage. They often win, but do not adequately publicize their achievements. Unions can use this opportunity to gain new members and retain existing ones, but only if companies don't take the initiative and liberalize their policies toward love at work.

CHAPTER 10
Avoiding and Ending Relationships

Love at work is becoming more complex as women are moving into higher-level positions. They're usually the peers rather than the subordinates of the men they encounter. Romantic opportunities are increasing, but so are the pitfalls, making thoughtful planning more important than ever. Some relationships develop into marriage while others break up, so prepare for both possibilities.

AVOIDING RELATIONSHIPS YOU DON'T WANT

You don't want a relationship with everyone, but saying "no" is sometimes difficult when you work together. Some relationships just happen. If you don't want a relationship, these are ten techniques you should use to keep it from happening:

1. Get to know him well, especially his faults.

2. Avoid terms of endearment, even "honey" or "dear."

3. Don't meet with him too frequently, especially after

others have left. Keep meetings brief, and include another person if you can.

4. If you must meet with him alone, keep the office door wide open.

5. Avoid being too close physically. Stand at arm's length or sit in a chair that accommodates only one.

6. Limit your conversations to business topics and public topics. Don't discuss personal matters or reveal emotions.

7. Discuss sexual harassment cases.

8. Don't tease him with your body language. Sit straight and carry yourself as if the big boss were present.

9. Keep him and yourself swamped with work.

10. Don't dress in a provocative manner, minimize perfume and makeup.

AVOIDING RELATIONSHIPS— WHOSE RESPONSIBILITY?

Sexual attraction is natural, but it isn't desired by everyone under all circumstances. Where does that leave the person who wants to go to work and be free from this type of interplay? What about the woman—or man—who doesn't want to flirt? You shouldn't be blamed when you're interested and the other person isn't, unless they've put you on notice.

In ancient times, such as 4 B.C. or the 1950s, people used various devices to ward off advances they found unwelcome. The most significant of these devices is the wedding ring. Why shouldn't people at work who want to be left alone wear a wedding ring? Even a nun wears one. If that amulet isn't powerful enough, a woman who doesn't want male attention could wear a habit, while a man who spurns female attention could wear Pilgrim garb or a monk's robe.

HOW TO REJECT A MAN'S ADVANCES

You don't want to have a relationship with every man you meet on your job or through your job. How can you turn off the men you don't want without turning off the man you want?

If a man asks you out, and you don't want him, reject the date but not him. Ego bruising can impair your future work relationship with him. Use an excuse that leaves his feelings intact. One idea you can use is "Paul, you know I like you very much, but I know we could never get seriously involved. Let's not jeoparadize our jobs for a relationship that will always be casual." Don't be nasty, especially if you want others to approach you.

How to Say "No"

You can reject a man's advances and keep on working with him as a co-worker. You make it easier for men if you make your real attitudes apparent. It's your privilege not to be bothered.

Here are some ways to say no:

- No, I'm married—and faithful.

- No, I'm not interested in a relationship right now.

- No, I'm seeing someone else exclusively.

- No, I like working with you, but I know enough about you to know we're not compatible.

- No, I'm too busy with this job plus my kids and school.

How to Say "Yes"

If you are interested, you can indicate approachability by statements such as:

- The guys where I work are terrific.

- I'd rather date someone I met at work. These days that's safer.

- I hate eating lunch alone.

How to Say "Maybe"

- I'm too busy this weekend, but would you give me a rain check?

- I'd like to know a little more about you first.

AVOIDANCE STRATEGIES

Avoiding Repeat Invitations

If a man is at all normal, and you say "no" firmly, he won't keep asking. Normal men fear rejection, especially in public. Discourage repeat invitations by rejecting him firmly but politely. When he asks you out the first time, just say "no"—and mean it. He'll feel humiliated if his co-workers know about the rejection, so reject him privately, at least the first time.

Repeat invitations from a man who doesn't interest you can be quite annoying, yet they're usually preventable. Suppose a man asks you out once or twice a week during a five-year period. It may not seem like much, but that's about four hundred invitations, which is clearly repetitious and annoying.

If your rejection sounds like a postponement, he may feel you have some interest in him and he may try again. Not every man can take a hint. If you show him partial acceptance, you might be leading him on inadvertently. Don't let him become obsessed with you.

A man who had an unhappy childhood may expect overwhelming rejection. He's had so much rejection that he just expects more. Your limited acceptances may provide his glimmer of hope, so of course he keeps on asking.

Keeping a Co-worker as a Friend

Why is it difficult to keep men as friends? Male–female friendship is sometimes an intermediate step toward love, but in the work context, you might want to keep friendship as friendship.

The primary reason why friendship turns into love is that friends tell the stories of their lives. When a man has an empathetic female listener, he retells his tales and relives the emotions attached to his stories. These long dormant emotions that he relives are invested in the empathetic listener, and before he knows it, he's in love with his listener.

A man will invest his emotions in you if you refrain from interrupting or censoring him. To prevent the relationship from developing, be sure to speak up and pass judgment on his actions. Compete with his stories, so that if he tells you that he won a scholarship, tell him about the one you won. You can even break his train of thought by chuckling a bit at some of his serious moments. If you balance just the right amount of censorship, competition, and criticism with otherwise empathetic listening, you'll sustain friendship but keep the romantic emotion in check and keep him at arm's length.

Another strategy you can use to keep the man as a friend is to treat him as an ordinary person. Virtually every normal man believes that he is different from other men—

that no one else is quite like him. If you want nothing more than friendship, let the man know that you don't find him truly unique, wonderful, or special.

Consequences of Avoiding the Relationship

Having a relationship can cause problems, but so can avoiding the relationship. If you and a potential lover avoid an affair, you may become upset by your mutual attraction and your affection may turn to hostility. Bear this risk in mind before you preclude the relationship, but if you're going to repress your sexual desire for him, focus on your differences in values and goals and on his negative features instead of his positive ones.

IF YOU SPLIT UP

Working with someone you love can be exhilarating, but working with a former lover can be extremely painful, especially if the breakup was bitter. It's distasteful to you and disruptive to the company, so try to stop working together when it hurts to see the other person.

When a relationship is close, you exchange a great deal of personal information and learn the other person's true personality and behavior. If you break up, the other person could use that insight and information to harm your career, so that's another reason to put some distance between you.

If you have to continue working together, your work relationship becomes extremely strained. Your co-workers will find the situation hard to deal with. Since they don't know what to say, they may avoid speaking to you. On a business level, they might not bring you together, even if they need to confer with both of you.

Some people feel that they *can't* be around the other person, especially if the relationship was intense or they're still attracted to each other. They may try to get rid of the other person by sabotaging the person's work or spreading vicious rumors. Be prepared to move on or defend yourself.

Torrid love affairs that break up don't immediately become placid friendships. Continued contact with him may be uncomfortable at first, but you may be able to work together in a normal manner and become pleasant to each other after a while.

How to Forget Him

If your romance goes sour and you must continue working with your former lover, you can insulate yourself from unpleasant thoughts that his presence continually stirs up. You'll alleviate some of the pain by redirecting your thoughts into your work or other relationships. Don't dwell on the past, especially if you were dumped. Start by enlisting the help of your friends, especially your other co-workers. You don't even have to tell them how they're helping you.

Your fellow has many qualities you enjoyed and now miss. Let's say that he was witty, a good storyteller, handsome, and a gourmet cook. It's tough to find that combination of qualities in just one person, but it's relatively easy to find each quality in different people. Spend your social office time with people who offer just one of his qualities you are missing. Spend the lunch hour with a companion who is a storyteller, take a coffee break with a witty companion, say hello to the most handsome men around you and teach them to respond in kind, and take up gourmet cooking. Since you're looking for only one attribute per person, you'll be finding people who are far superior in that context to your former lover, and he'll be easier to forget.

Divorce

If you are married to each other when you break up, the problems are even more severe than if you are just lovers. First, you have to deal with the gossip. If you think people gossip about a relationship, think of how they gossip about a divorce.

The divorce decree chills the relationship, but it brings a sense of relief because of its finality. The divorce process has an even worse effect on the work relationship. If he has become your bitter enemy at home, this bitterness is likely to spill over into the office. If you can't keep your personal dispute out of the office, the company will have good grounds for firing both of you. To minimize the risks, avoid having your future ex-spouse served with divorce papers at the office. Don't demolish his desk or start cursing at him while you're in public.

Like it or not, you're in a lifeboat together even if you are going through a divorce. Don't try to see who can put bigger holes in a lifeboat that is already sinking. This is very hard advice to follow if passions are strong. If you can get through the divorce with some degree of class, then other men will be more comfortable about approaching you.

MOVING FORWARD

You may need to end your relationship with Mr. Wrong before you find and marry Mr. Right. The selection process has its unpleasant moments for you and him. Rejection and broken relationships are never pleasant, but the unpleasantness can be minimized if you're in a position, through work, where you must continue to respect each other as co-workers or colleagues. Ideally, you'll be able to make a minor job change and avoid contact with your former lover or encourage him to change jobs. Then you'll be in a better frame of mind to find Mr. Right.

CHAPTER 11

Working with Your Lover

Working together is great for some couples, but not for others. Some couples should work apart, some should work apart for the same company, and others should work together. In fact, some couples should go into business for themselves while others work as a couple-team for a larger business.

SHOULD YOU WORK WITH YOUR LOVER?

If you and your lover work for the same company, you might have too much in common, especially if you work in the same department. Close proximity causes happiness for some couples and boredom for others. Pretend for a moment that you're already married and think of the level of excitement you need for your own happiness. Most married people look forward to telling their spouses about "my day," but what if your day is also his day? If your job doesn't give you enough stimulus, you'll need to share the excitement from his job and gain emotional release from telling him about your day. If so, working together isn't for you unless you can get the excitement you need from recreation and hobbies.

WORKING APART FOR THE SAME COMPANY

You and your lover might enjoy working for the same company, but not working together. For you, the ideal situation is to work in departments that have little or no contact. He may be in accounting while you're in personnel. Or he's part of the consumer products division while you're with the industrial products division. Or perhaps you're in purchasing and he's in order processing. If you work with other people in different situations, you'll each bring these separate experiences into the relationship and benefit from the stimulus they provide.

GOING INTO BUSINESS WITH YOUR SPOUSE

An increasing number of people are going into business with their spouses. This arrangement presents unique opportunities for both success and fulfillment, but also can cause substantial business and marital problems.

If you're in love, the synergy may be propelling the two of you to great happiness and achievement. However, a business failure may destroy your relationship, and failure in your relationship is even more likely to destroy your business. If you and your lover are contemplating a partnership in both love and business, consider and resolve the following issues first.

Business and Personal Distinctions

Family members who are in business together are not necessarily equal partners. Work roles can be very different from family relationships. At work, one may be the direct superior of another. If you and your lover expect to be equal partners, specify this arrangement in your business contract. Since business and personal roles differ, family members who work in the same business need to signal when work ends and family life begins.

Financial Ups and Downs

When you and your lover work together, the ups and downs of the economy and successes and failures of the business affect both of you since you have your eggs in the same financial basket. The joys of victory and the agonies of defeat are highlighted and accentuated. You're less able to serve as buffers for each other against the world because you are both facing the same world. Your marital stress is likely to increase, but the stress might draw you closer together.

Childcare

If you and your lover will have children, plan for childcare, particularly during busy periods when both of you face business burdens. A good support system of other family members and friends can be crucial in solving these childcare problems.

Chores

Discuss the division of household chores in advance to avoid unpleasant surprises later. A sharing of work in the business is likely to lead to a sharing of work at home, but men usually do less than their proportionate share of household tasks. Eat out often and hire household help if you can to save time and energy for both business and personal activities.

Vacations

You and your lover prefer to vacation together, but joint vacations are difficult or even impossible when you both work together in a small business. Often, a husband and wife who work together forgo their vacations until their business grows. Thus for a number of years, they'll lose out on the personal renewal that a vacation brings. If you're too busy for regular vacations, take short vacations as part of your business trips.

Boredom

Living and working with the same person can sometimes be boring, no matter how much you love each other. You'll limit the risk of boredom by maintaining close contact with others, whether by telephone or in person. Also, review your topics of conversation to see if they're repetitious. If so, broaden your horizons by visits to your local bookstore.

Workaholics and Their Lazy Spouses

You have an idea of how much time should be spent at work or in work-related activities, and so does your lover. However, your priorities are likely to differ because of the extent you enjoy work rather than other activities, your ego, your need for money, your energy level, and your long-term goals. The person who works harder calls the second person lazy. This second person calls the first a workaholic. As your relationship develops, compare your priorities with your lover's. Then consider carefully whether you can respect each other's priorities before you tie the knot.

COUPLES AS TEAMS

Some couples can work effectively as teams. If you and your lover are such a couple, and you enjoy working for others, work for a company that wants you to focus your energies on the same project.

Husband-and-wife teams can do some jobs better than two unrelated individuals, especially where long hours, extensive travel, and close contact are necessary. These include industrial sales, systems design, truck driving, and tax consulting. A husband–wife team can develop new products together, visit customers together, or see clients together. You and your lover may be such a team.

The number of couples working together has been increasing, and we expect this trend to continue. After you meet on your job or through your job, you'll probably enjoy working together.

CONCLUSION

You'll find that the benefits from working together are substantial, the drawbacks are minor, and you'll be successful in combining business and pleasure.